# The Art of On-the-Job Writing

## PHILIP VASSALLO

**FIRST BOOKS** ®

PORTLAND • OREGON

Author: Philip Vassallo

Editor: Linda Weinerman

Design and production: Masha Shubin

ISBN-13: 978-0-912301-62-4
ISBN-10: 0-912301-62-7

Printed in the USA

Published by First Books, 6750 SW Franklin Street, Portland, OR 97223-2542, USA, tel 503.968.6777, www.firstbooks.com

TO

Georgia Vassallo

*wife, mother, daughter, sister, aunt, cousin, friend, teacher*

# Table of Contents

# Acknowledgments

I am grateful to Jeremy Solomon, President of First Books, who encouraged me to write the first edition of *The Art of On-the-Job Writing* in 2002 and who so graciously decided to publish its second edition. A special thanks goes to Linda Weinerman, First Books editor extraordinaire, whose helpful suggestions and face-saving corrections (yes, we could all use good editors) have made the book better than it otherwise would have been. I am also grateful to Masha Shubin, First Books graphic designer, whose work for the book aptly illustrates what visuals do for words.

Since many of the ideas in this book have emerged from years of teaching, writing, and assessing writing during a consulting career which has given me great joy, I should express my indebtedness to Paul Dennithorne Johnston, Editor of *ETC: A Review of General Semantics*; Jeremy Klein, Consulting Editor of *ETC*; and Steven Stockdale, Executive Director of the Institute of General Semantics. Since 1992, they have supported my **Words on the Line** column, from which the book sprung. I thank Michael Bartlett for his professional and spiritual guidance. In addition, so many clients, students, and friends too numerous to mention here have informed much of what appears in this book. I recall them with deep gratitude as I write these words.

I express my gratitude to the memory of my father, Frank Vassallo, who showed me the importance of reading; the memory of my mother, Lucy Vassallo, who encouraged my reading; my sister, Elizabeth Hitz, who was my first model of successful writing and teaching; my brother, Abel Vassallo, who was my first model of efficient reading; my brother-in-law, John Hitz, who pointed me to many great writers; my wife, Georgia, who has always supported my creative endeavors; and my daughters, Elizabeth and Helen, on whose behalf I've dedicated my career.

Finally and foremost, I thank God, Who *is* the Word, and without Whom I would not have had this time—and a good time it has been.

# INTRODUCTION

I have written *The Art of On-the-Job Writing* after teaching business and technical writing in colleges and corporations for more than a quarter century, after consulting to thousands of students and corporate executive, administrative, and technical staff, and after reading, evaluating, editing, and writing thousands of workplace documents. I have written this book because I maintain two strong beliefs about writing for the workplace:

1. On-the-job writing relies on creativity and artistry just as writing for the screen, stage, or bookstore does.
2. On-the-job writing can be learned by any employee through application of the systematic approach described in this book.

Many excellent business- and technical-writing books are available at your bookstore and online, and my intent is not to compete with those that offer numerous models of good writing, illustrations of grammar problems, and exercises on writing situations. *The Art of On-the-Job Writing* offers something different: an integrated method for achieving workplace-writing success. It accomplishes this by providing you with four critical tools:

1. The elements of the PDQ on-the-job *writing process* (planning, drafting, quality controlling).

2. The four pillars of the on-the-job *writing product*, which I call the 4S Plan (statement, support, structure, style).
3. The techniques to move academic writers from the polemic, *me*-focused style of essay writing to the more results-oriented, *us*-focused style of business writing and *it*-focused style of technical writing.
4. The groundwork for becoming and staying a successful on-the-job writer through a description of inspirational, memorable, and relevant writing tips.

You've picked up the right book if you're looking for a fast read or a studied read of workplace writing. If you're on the run, you will get quick ideas on:

· improving your workplace creativity
· writing with a powerful sense of purpose
· discovering ways to better understand the people who read your documents
· organizing your ideas for maximum impact
· writing drafts quickly and painlessly
· checking that your drafts are consistent, complete, clear, concise, and courteous
· editing your drafts for proper sentence structure, expressive vocabulary, and correct grammar
· proofreading your document to catch all your mistakes

But if you're looking for a book that presents an in-depth analysis of writing challenges common to most corporate employees, you will find plenty to read about. The case studies that run through Chapters 2, 3, and 4 will keep your interest, as will the numerous practice opportunities in Chapters 4, 5, and 6. You will benefit from the book's structured approach to writing, one that will become your own when you have finished reading it. Enjoy the learning.

# CHAPTER 1

# Being an On-the-Job Writer

"Always dream and shoot higher than you know you can do. Don't bother just to be better than your contemporaries or predecessors. Try to be better than yourself."

— William Faulkner, 1956, New York City, from
*Writers at Work: The Paris Review Interviews*

This chapter describes what you should know and have for successful on-the job writing. It comprises four general sections: 1) an introduction to the challenges that writers face when composing documents on the job, 2) an overview of the writing *process*, 3) a description of the writing *product*, and 4) a discussion of the tools of the on-the-job writer's trade.

## The Road to Success Starts with Knowing the Challenges Ahead

In the past two decades, I have trained thousands of business and technical writers, some fresh out of college just learning to write on the job, and others experienced businesspeople who for many years have communicated successfully and now find themselves in a new job or field with different and challenging writing requirements. Some appear content with their job, others miserable. Some have no job at all, and still others strive to move across or up the corporation or pursue a business of their own. Some flaunt an impressive flair for written expression and easily compose documents on demand, while others struggle with a vocabulary so limited that they feel inhibited to write even a sentence. Still others speak English as a second, third, or fourth language, some of them with remarkable fluency and others with great difficulty. (These writers, recent arrivals in the United States from south of the border or across the Atlantic or Pacific, often comprise the majority of students in my writing classes.) In recent years, the ubiquity of worldwide electronic communication has created situations in which I never meet in person some of my students, who may be an Indian on the opposite American coast, or a Chinese in London, or an American in Hong Kong, all grappling with communication issues that conflict with their host culture. Some have a limited formal education but write clearly, concisely, and correctly, while others hold advanced degrees yet remain weak in organizing their ideas on paper.

Regardless of the course's difficulty level or the students' experience level, I will occasionally hear a student state as a course goal, "I want to write what I have to say the first time around without needing to revise the document."

Wouldn't we all!

But here on Planet Earth, in the modern office—with all its electronic, environmental, and personal distractions—no one can reasonably expect important documents to materialize flawlessly in a single mental bound. Good writing emerges from rewriting—even in the fast-paced, no-nonsense, no-excuses corporate world.

A well-written report, proposal, instruction manual, or even e-mail demands that writers attend to numerous matters of logic, syntax, and diction in spite of the high-pressure environment in which they find themselves. Those issues, among many others, remain at the forefront of the careful writer's quality-control checklist—and they confuse the inexperienced writer. Just review any excellent business, technical, or scientific writing stylebook. They generally run hundreds of pages for good reason. The punch list of language issues is long enough to make learning it a lifelong project.

How then, with all these potential problems and pitfalls looming over your psyche, do you possibly become a better writer? You can start right here. No question about it. Whether you are an administrative assistant, manager, technical support person, scientist, engineer, or executive, you can become a better writer. This book will go a long way toward helping you understand what you need to practice the on-the-job writing craft. It will empower you with a clear, concise, memorable writing method, one that will enable you to improve your writing skills for as long as you remain committed to that goal.

Before getting started toward becoming a more efficient (speed) and effective (quality) writer, understand the first principle of on-the-job writing: Writing is a *process* as well as a *product*. The process is the *how* of writing, the means by which you complete the document; the product is the *what* of writing, the finished document. The process is your labor, the product your fruit; the process is your transportation, the product your destination. The rest of this chapter talks about the process and the product of writing and the tools you need to master your on-the-job writing assignments. Let's get started!

## The Writing Process

So where should you start? A brief overview of the writing process—the mental and physical activities that occur while you actually write—may serve useful here. We'll start with the mnemonic PDQ: Planning, Drafting, Quality Controlling. Most of us know these initials stand for Pretty Darn Quick, so the initials serve a good purpose because the PDQ writing process will help you write faster. Relatively few of us have the title of "writer" on our job, yet more than ever, we must write frequently and quickly, often juggling multiple writing tasks, some of them in collaboration with office teammates, some completely solo, and some for other people's signature (like our boss's or our client's). Still we loathe the idea of calling ourselves writers.

Why? Because we have other things to do: attend meetings, follow up on them, and plan for the next one; call clients, vendors, managers, subordinates, or teammates; research data on spreadsheets and on the Internet; read reports, articles, letters, memos, and e-mails; troubleshoot problems that we worked so hard to avoid; purchase, sell, or return office items; attend seminars and brief our managers on what we accomplished at them; and many more tasks, some mundane and others monumental, but all revolving around keeping the business moving full-speed ahead. The last thing we want to do is write anything that we really don't have to.

PDQ—planning, drafting, quality controlling—helps us to make writing easy and efficient. Again, we must remember that writing is a *process* as well as a *product*. The *product* is what appears on the printed page: your memos, letters, reports, instructions, and proposals, among many other documents that you may write. What you are reading at this moment is a writing *product*. You can judge the quality of the writing *product*; however, you cannot judge the quality of the writing *process* because you did not watch me write these words. As I said earlier, the writing process includes the mental and physical activities occurring while you actually write. The last document you wrote is a *product*; what it took you to complete it is the *process*.

The distinction between the two is a critical one. Frequently, I meet clients who write outstanding documents. They clearly deliver their point, precisely organize their supporting details, and carefully craft polished sentences. However, they may struggle through the first draft, rewriting their first sentence many times over before getting into a "writer's groove," or they may experience stress to the point of nausea while they labor through the draft, or they may procrastinate several hours—and sometimes days—before getting started. In these cases, the writers are strong on *product* and weak on *process*; they're effective but not efficient. On the other end, I also meet writers who breeze through the planning and drafting stages but end up with documents that are purposeless, disorganized, or grammatically flawed. In these cases, the writers appear strong on *process* (but not really because they didn't effectively quality control the document) and weak on *product*. On the job, we want to be strong in both product and process to best serve our readers and ourselves. So here we go: PDQ—**p**lan, **d**raft, **q**uality control.

## Step 1: Planning

Planning, the first step of the writing process, embodies the brainstorming and organizing tasks that writers perform to overcome writer's block and generate ideas. Considering the purpose of the document and the intended audience, writers randomly list and then deliberately assemble the details to appear in the draft. Of course, this description seems too ineffectual for writers composing lengthier documents, such as a 10-page executive summary, 20-page product description, 40-page annual report, 80-page formal proposal, or 160-page root-cause analysis. These writers need to plan in a more substantial way, researching, evaluating, and selecting voluminous data, interviewing sources, and discussing documentation strategies with teammates, to mention a few tasks. A description of the many ways in which writers actually plan before drafting appears in Chapter 2. Suffice to say for now, we plan our drafts—either on the computer or on paper—to stir the creative juices, to trigger the imagination, to transform the nebulous images floating in our effervescent, multitasking brain into words on a page.

## Step 2: Drafting

With a plan before them, writers ideally tear through a rough draft, the second step of the writing process. This does not necessarily mean that they start with the first sentence and end with the last, nor does it mean that they start with a blank screen or page. A *Wall Street Journal* article by Barbara Jepson suggests that the composing process of certain musicians may ring true for wordsmiths. She writes that composer Krzysztof Penderecki "starts his work in the middle, to avoid the kind of writer's block that can occur when a composer [confronts] a blank piece of manuscript paper. [Composer Wolfgang Rihm creates] on used manuscript paper to overcome the same problem." Understanding that criticism compromises creativity, writers move through the draft without changing ideas or correcting mistakes. Here, they prefer quantity to quality, wanting nothing more than the content for the quality control step of the writing process. In effect, they do Steps 1 and 2 only for themselves, and they do Step 3 for the intended readers. Chapter 3 focuses on the drafting stage.

## Step 3: Quality Controlling

When quality controlling, we protect our REP: **r**evise, **e**dit, and **p**roofread, in that order, for efficiency's sake. In short, we revise the ideas of the document, edit the expression of language, and proofread the hard copy for mistakes. Each of these quality-controlling responsibilities imposes distinguishable tasks on the writer. (Table 1-1 shows a way of dividing some of these tasks.)

The order in which we complete these tasks matters greatly. Why, for instance, would we sharpen the quality of a sentence (an editing chore) only to later discard altogether the idea expressed in it (a revising chore)? Or why would we fuss over the consistency of spacing between sections of report (a proofreading task) only to later redesign the report without sections (revising)?

When revising, writers CARE, **c**hanging, **a**dding, **r**eorganizing or **r**eformatting, and **e**liminating their ideas at the service of their purpose and audience. They check that each paragraph contains only one complete idea and that their ideas connect logically from one paragraph to the next. They decide whether employing headings would efficiently guide the reader through dense or complex material, and whether using bullets or numbers would effectively focus the reader on key points and eliminate unnecessary or repetitious words. Revising obligates us to rethink our focus, develop our points in greater detail, determine the best possible order for conveying our message, and delete points that may distract the reader from capturing the essence of our document. Many experts agree that revising challenges us with the most critical moment of writing because it represents our last chance to show the reader precisely what we think. This book covers revising in greater depth in Chapter 4.

## TABLE 1-1
## THE QUALITY CONTROLLING SYSTEM

| Quality Controlling | Checking For | Some Tasks |
|---|---|---|
| Revising | Ideas:<br>• paragraphs<br>• headings<br>• bullets<br>• graphics | • change<br>• add<br>• reorganize/reformat<br>• eliminate |
| Editing | Language:<br>• sentences<br>• words | • sentence structure<br>• voice<br>• tone<br>• conciseness<br>• parallelism<br>• modification<br>• diction<br>• punctuation<br>• mechanics |
| Proofreading | Mistakes | • headings, footers, and margins, spacing<br>• font consistency<br>• common errors<br>• typos |

When editing, we concern ourselves with the structure, conciseness, and clarity of our sentences as well as the correctness and appropriateness of our word usage and punctuation. After painstakingly crystallizing and aligning our ideas to suit our purpose, we would not want sloppy sentences, garbled grammar, or wasted words to distract the reader from understanding what we mean. While overriding style issues may occur to us during revision, we may seek to eliminate unnecessary passive voice or guard against shifts in tone during editing. Of course, myriad other matters cross our mind at this point. For word variety, we may fiddle with the thesaurus feature of our writing software. We may read our sentences aloud to hear how they will "sound" to the reader, knowing that if we run out of breath mid-sentence or stumble over our words, so will our readers lose their train of thought while reading silently. Reading aloud also hones the writer's punctuating skills because of the strong link between intonation in speaking and punctuation in writing. Chapter 5 reviews the many aspects of editing.

When proofreading, it's best to have a hard copy in hand, which revising and editing do not necessarily require of us. We may easily modify the idea of a paragraph or change the syntax of a sentence while reading from a monitor, but we will find proofreading (reading a proof) easier while reading the document as it will appear to the reader. Here we check for consistency in spacing and font type, style, and size; correctness of footers and headers; common errors such as misspelled names, mistyped numbers, and incorrect homonyms; and a whole host of other details that even the most experienced writers and their editors may overlook. Haven't you ever been surprised when a reader glancing cursorily at one of your documents immediately spots a typo in a paragraph that you meticulously labored over? It happens—so we proofread, which is covered in Chapter 6.

## Using PDQ Efficiently

Now that you have an overview of the writing process, you may reasonably wonder, "Isn't doing all this stuff going to take me longer to complete a document? The answer is no, not if you use the process thoughtfully. You do not have to submit *all* your documents to such a rigorous method—only those documents challenging you the most. You wouldn't spend a minute writing a one-sentence e-mail, but you would likely spend many hours crafting, say, an annual report. Knowing the writing process and using it will keep you on track while composing that more challenging document.

One way of deciding when to use the complete writing process—planning, drafting, quality controlling—becomes clear once you consider that busy on-the-job writers face three levels of complexity in their writing tasks, depending on their experience with the assignment. These levels—routine, regulated, and reflective—cover any writing that comes across your desk.

## Level 1: Routine Writing

This kind of writing comes easy to the writer, almost as naturally as speech. Examples may include handwritten notes that you compose for yourself or others or brief e-mails, memos, or letters that you create daily, such as routine requests or responses to requests. Attention to detail and grammatical conventions does not seem to matter so much in routine writing because you've done this document so often that you know it works for you and your readers. When writing routine documents, you won't waste your time planning (Step 1 of the writing process), and you spend little or no time quality controlling (Step 3); therefore, you only need to draft (Step 2).

## Level 2: Regulated Writing

This level brings greater challenges to the writer. It demands more detail and attention to the task, but the writer can follow established formats and easily retrieve content from memory, files, or other sources. Examples may include employee appraisals, meeting minutes, and status reports.

You know you are writing regulated documents when you don't have to generate and organize your ideas—challenging tasks for most writers—because the outline is built into the document. You may just have to fill in blanks or answer questions. You may use a template (standard format) or borrow from boilerplate (phrases and passages that you've used repeatedly). You need not spend any time on planning; however, since the document is rich with detail and may reach many readers, you would want to spend time quality controlling it for content accuracy and grammatical correctness. Therefore, this level of writing calls for you to draft and quality control.

## Level 3: Reflective Writing

This level poses the greatest challenge to the writer because it requires a high level of thinking about the purpose, supporting details, organization, format, and style, some or all of which may not be readily apparent to the writer. Often the demands of the audience create problems for the writer; other times, the writer's lack of knowledge or information about the topic creates additional challenges. Examples of reflective writing may include proposals to readers inside or outside the company, technical requirements or reports, standard operating procedures, and company-wide directives or policy announcements.

You know that your writing is on the reflective level when you enter the writing task uncertain about what it should say or how it should look or who the readers will be. You know that your document templates and boilerplate will not do for the particular task. You also know that grammar and usage and tone issues will play a more critical part than usual in how readers receive your document. All of that stuff about proper English that you learned in school will matter too. In reflective writing, you need to plan, draft, and quality control the document.

These three levels appear in Table 1-2 in order of increasing complexity. To understand the distinctions among these levels, think about the level in which you would place particular documents that you write. Also, note two points:

- The examples in the table are purely subjective; what may be easy for one writer may be challenging for another.
- You should be able to place into each level at least one of your own writing assignments.

**TABLE 1-2**
**THREE LEVELS OF COMPLEXITY**
**OF ON-THE-JOB WRITING**

| Level | Description | Possible Examples |
|-------|-------------|-------------------|
| Routine | Easy writing requiring little or no planning or quality controlling. | • handwritten notes<br>• brief e-mails<br>• routine requests<br>• routine responses |
| Regulated | More detailed writing requiring little planning because the writer can choose established formats and select content from memory, files, or other sources. | • staff and self-appraisals<br>• meeting minutes<br>• status reports |
| Reflective | The most complex writing requiring a high level of thinking about the purpose, details, organization, format, and style, some or all of which may not be readily apparent. | • proposals<br>• operating procedures<br>• company briefings |

Remember that professional writers follow certain guidelines when approaching these different levels of complexity:

- They draft their *routine* documents right away, often bunching up those easy writing tasks over brief periods that do not require their greatest level of attention. Some experienced writers claim that they can write these documents even when they are on the phone or engaged in some other task.

- They refer to prescribed formats and whatever written resources they have at their disposal to compose *regulated* documents.
- They carefully plan their *reflective* documents using a dependable method (the focus of Chapter 2). In doing so, they easily overcome writer's block and get their ideas flowing.

Understanding the writing process and levels of on-the-job writing complexity will achieve at least five benefits for you and the people and company you write for:

1. You will better see distinctions between academic writing, which is often theoretical, argumentative, and personal, and on-the-job writing, which is results driven and audience focused; therefore, you will employ the writing process appropriate to your purpose and your reader's needs.
2. You will be less likely to procrastinate over writing assignments because you will know how to get started. And even when you do procrastinate, you will at least know why and what to do about it.
3. You will experience less writing-related stress because you will be capable of purposeful, organized, clear, concise, and correct writing—without necessarily being a widely published author or an expert in grammar.
4. You will be better able to track your progress on any of your writing projects because your method allows you to divide your assignments into discrete phases.
5. You will feel more confident and accomplished because you are using the tools and techniques that professional writers use.

## The Writing Product

As on-the-job *readers*, most people know what to look for in quality documents; as on-the-job *writers*, however, they often become ambivalent about quality. As readers, we think nothing of mentally sidestepping a memo or report that we find uninteresting or confusing. We may judge the writer's weak approach to the subject or inattention to language standards, but for the most part we simply brush aside the document as useless, inadequate, or irrelevant. Our thinking is the opposite when we are writing. We want to do whatever we can to ensure that our reader gets the point as completely, clearly, concisely, and correctly as possible. Here lies a good place to begin thinking about the writing *product*: identify those elements we look for as readers, and apply them to what we want to achieve as writers.

# The "4S" Plan

The four most critical domains of a well-written document are the *4S Plan*: *statement*, *support*, *structure*, and *style*. They conveniently cover the key elements of excellent writing. Regardless of the type of writing, writers must plan their documents (Step 1) and quality control them (Step 3) mindful of the *statement*, *support*, *structure*, and *style*.

## The Statement

The *statement*, or the point of the document, represents the writer's purpose. It is the vision, the mission statement of the document. It is the one sentence that speaks for the entire document. The *statement* should actually appear in the document, usually at the beginning. Table 1-3 shows some examples of the *statement*.

### TABLE 1-3
### THE STATEMENT

| Document | Statement |
|---|---|
| instructions | This document describes the procedure for operating and maintaining the XYZ machine. |
| employee recommendation | I am pleased to offer a recommendation for Tina Sakacs as your administrative assistant. |
| meeting minutes | Below are the minutes of the Quality Control Team's June 6 meeting. |
| internal proposal | To ensure optimal productivity during the evening shift, I propose that our group retain a maintenance technician for the injection molding equipment. |
| policy directive | Effective September 28, all office staff must prominently display their Company picture ID. |
| creditor reminder | We ask that you refer to our most recent invoice, for which we have not yet received payment. |

The *statement* may seem too obvious to merit any serious attention; however, many writers tend to write a letter of complaint without clearly stating what they expect their reader to do, focusing on the problem and never looking toward the solution. Other writers may state a business threat to their manager without proposing any clear course of action. Still others lose touch with what they have to say because they have never articulated their one-sentence *statement*. This is what we mean by "reinventing the wheel" and "spinning your wheels." Purposeful writers—those with a clear vision of their *statement*—keep their purpose in mind. They know that readers want to discover the statement even *before* they read the document; the *statement* is what motivates the audience to read the details. We cannot manage a document through the writing process without a clear *statement*.

In addition to placing their statement up front, purposeful writers also close with clear next steps, which advance the purpose. Next steps are the reader's transition from the document. In other words, the *statement* tells what the document is about, and the *next steps* tell the reader what will happen next in relation to that statement. Next steps are not throwaway lines or some awkward closing for lack of anything better to write; they are thoughtful expressions that advance the purpose statement in its fullest sense. Examples of next steps appear in Table 1-4.

### The Support

The *support*, or details, is the information that bolsters the statement. The *support* gives the reader the reasons for the writer's *statement*. It is what the reader needs to know about the statement. The *statement* makes the point, and the *support* supplies the details. To understand how the *statement* and *support* collaborate, consider the examples in Table 1-5.

A common question that even good writers struggle to answer is, "How much detail should I include to support my purpose?" You will find the answer to that question by considering your readers—both the primary and the secondary readers:

- *Primary* readers are the persons to whom you addressed the message.
- *Secondary* readers are the persons you've copied and others to whom the primary readers or you may send a copy. They may be the primary readers' or the writer's subordinates, peers, managers, clients, vendors, or others who they believe are appropriate recipients of the message.

## TABLE 1-4
## THE PURPOSE STATEMENT WITH THE NEXT STEPS

| Document | Purpose Statement | Next Steps |
|---|---|---|
| instructions | This document describes the procedure for operating and maintaining the XYZ machine. | If operators have any question concerning the safe and efficient procedure for operating and maintaining the XYZ machine, they should refer to the troubleshooting guide in this manual or call Quality Control at extension 406. |
| employee recommendation | I am pleased to offer a recommendation for Tina Sakacs as your administrative assistant. | I believe that Ms. Sakacs's skills and diligence would contribute significantly to your organization, and I welcome any question you may have about her qualifications. |
| meeting minutes | Below are the minutes of the Quality Control Team's June 6 meeting. | The Team will meet again on July 19 at 9:00 a.m. in Conference Room A. |
| internal proposal | To ensure optimal productivity during the evening shift, I propose that our group retain a maintenance technician for the injection molding equipment. | Upon your approval, I would be happy to draft a job description and begin the hiring process for this critical position. |
| policy directive | Effective September 28, all office staff must prominently display their Company picture ID. | Your compliance with this policy will ensure that our Company is doing all it can to address security concerns. |
| creditor reminder | We ask that you refer to our most recent invoice, for which we have not yet received payment. | Please remit payment in full by August 21 or call us before that date if you have any question about the invoice. |

Therefore, the *context* of a message plays a huge role in determining the *content*.

· *Content*: the information contained in the document.

· *Context*: the situation that created the need for the document, and the relationship of the writer to the reader.

Chapters 2 through 4 cover the crucial considerations about knowing your primary and secondary readers as well as determining the *content* by understanding the *context*.

## The Structure

The *structure* is the organization and format of the document. "Listening" to the *statement*, the *structure* examines the *support*, ordering and shaping it in a way that best reinforces the *statement*. *Structure* is the builder of the document. It assembles all the parts so that they stand up as one whole. *Support* tells the information that the reader needs to know, and *structure* determines the order in which the reader gets the information.

This is not to say that *structure* is nothing more than an enumerator. It is also the place in the *4S Plan* where the writer decides which details are unnecessary, which require elaboration, and which can be combined as single points. The *structure* would look at the *support* in Table 1-5 and determine the method of development while focused on the *statement*. Examples of methods of development appear in Table 1-6 (page 18). Writers who consider method of development in the planning and drafting steps of the writing process often find that their documents require less quality controlling than if they had started without a clear direction.

The *structure* calls for other organizational devices as well. They include the ODC (opening-discussion-closing), Paragraph IQ (idea-qualification), and format (headings, bullets, illustrations)—all of which make excellent quality control tools.

### Opening-Discussion-Closing (ODC)

The ODC emerges from the logical pattern by which we express ideas in a purposeful, focused dialogue. All formal documents have an ODC:

· Opening—the purpose statement and the preview of the details to follow
· Discussion—the details supporting the purpose statement
· Closing—the review of the details and the next steps

Each point clearly connects from one to the other, and each depends on the other to create a unified whole for the reader.

**TABLE 1-5**
**THE SUPPORT**

| Statement | Support |
|---|---|
| This document describes the procedure for operating and maintaining the XYZ machine. | • intended user<br>• intended purpose of XYZ machine<br>• description of technical terms<br>• description of machine parts<br>• operating guide, step-by-step<br>• maintenance guide, step-by-step<br>• troubleshooting guide |
| I am pleased to offer a recommendation for Tina Sakacs as your administrative assistant. | • how I know her<br>• her productivity<br>• her dependability<br>• her integrity<br>• her knowledge |
| Below are the minutes of the Quality Control Committee's June 6 meeting. | • members attending<br>• Project 101 update<br>• problems with new gluing machine<br>• travel itinerary for Chicago trip<br>• next meeting |
| To ensure optimal productivity during the evening shift, I propose that our group retain a maintenance technician for the injection molding equipment. | • recent problems with equipment breakdown<br>• production and cost impact of problems<br>• cost of installing a technician<br>• responsibilities of technician<br>• intended results of installing technician |
| Effective September 28, all office staff must prominently display their Company picture ID. | • need for improved security<br>• where, when, and how ID should be displayed<br>• instructions for those who have no ID |
| We ask that you refer to our most recent invoice, for which we have not yet received payment. | • appreciation for being a loyal customer<br>• invoice number, date, and amount<br>• days past due<br>• apology if payment has been sent<br>• courteous close |

## TABLE 1-6
## METHODS OF DEVELOPMENT

| Method | Description | Example |
|---|---|---|
| Enumeration | a numerical listing of supporting details, usually in a specific order | PDAs have had a positive impact on the MNO Corporation for seven reasons. |
| Chronological | a chronological listing of supporting details | Here are the milestones in the development of the enhancements to the MNO Corporation's PDA system since initiating it in 2002. |
| Spatial | a geographically or spatially arranged listing of supporting details | The following is a description of the PDA's features as they appear on the screen. |
| General-to-Specific | a broad-to-narrow, or general-to-specific, listing of the supporting details | The PDA has improved the MNO Corporation—from its industry-wide image to its employees' communication efficiency. |
| Specific-to-General | a narrow-to-broad, or specific-to-general, listing of the supporting details | The PDA has solved the MNO Corporation's major communication problems—from tracking lost orders in the shipping department to apprising Board Members of breaking developments in the field. |
| Advantages-Disadvantages | a division of supporting details based on advantages and disadvantages | MNO's latest PDA upgrades have both improved wireless e-mailing capability and created new communication problems. |
| Similarities-Differences | a division of supporting details based on similarities and differences | MNO's new PDA both mirrors and differs from its earlier version. |
| Problem-Solution | a division of supporting details starting with a discussion of the problem, the method of resolving it, and the results of applying the method | To solve the problem of overuse of jamming PDAs with excessive e-mail, MNO has tried blocking particular e-mail addresses throughout the network; this resulted in a 12 percent decrease in receiving external junk e-mail. |

## Paragraph Idea-Qualification (IQ)

The Paragraph IQ looks at the paragraphs within the details for emphasis and unity, ensuring that each paragraph states one idea, and that each following sentence qualifies it. The first sentence, sometimes called a topic sentence, states the big idea of the paragraph. The following sentences support the idea sentence—just as the details of the entire document support the purpose statement. They qualify the point, usually by restricting, expanding, or illustrating it:

- Restriction—The qualifying sentences restrict the meaning of the idea by limiting its definition.
- Expansion—The qualifying sentences expand the meaning of the idea by broadening its definition.
- Illustration—The qualifying sentences illustrate the meaning of the idea by providing a single example or multiple examples of it.

## Format

Finally, format provides clearly and consistently structured headings, bullets, and illustrations, such as tables, charts, and graphs to guide readers through the ideas of the document. It offers the readers a high-level view of the writer's method of development and supporting ideas so that the readers could achieve three desired outcomes:

- scan the document for the big ideas and their supporting points
- capture just the information they need
- respond to the writer more efficiently and effectively

Chapter 4 reviews all of these organizational devices in detail.

## The Style

What would the document manager (*statement*) with a strong worker (*support*) and a focused builder (*structure*) still need? An artist. Once visionary architects select building materials and design the building's structure, they still need an artistic touch to give the building a distinctive flourish, an aesthetic appeal. How much natural light will the building accept? What about the landscaping?

Such artistic notions would likely intimidate the hard-nosed, bottom-line–driven investment banker who creates equity research reports, or the empirically grounded scientist who writes dry lab findings, both of whom may feel that their field demands no-nonsense, straightforward talk. They happen to be right in claiming that their writing style should live in the black-and-white areas of language and steer clear of the colorful; however, they would be mistaken to dismiss any consideration of *style*. In fact, when technical and scientific writers speak of the need for formal and impersonal writing, they are speaking of *style*. Just as the art world's paintings range from the brilliant colors of Van Gogh to the stark black-and-white photorealist portraits of Chuck Close, just as the music world embraces rhythms ranging from hip-hop to Bach Baroque, so too does every type of business and technical writing have *style*.

*Style* goes far beyond reducing a document to a particular sense that it gives the reader: personal or impersonal, general or technical, informal or formal. It is the way we dress up our document. Here we decide how much *context* language should accompany the *content* language. Table 1-7 shows how awful our documents would "sound" without some *context* language.

### TABLE 1-7
### STYLE—"CONTENT" AND "CONTEXT" LANGUAGE

| "Content" Language Only | "Content" with "Context" Language |
|---|---|
| You have been promoted. | We are pleased to inform you that you have been promoted. |
| We must terminate your services. | We are sorry that we have to discontinue our working relationship. |
| Enclosed is the material you requested. | Thank you for requesting information about our product. We are happy to provide the enclosed material to help you in deciding whether to use our services. |
| If necessary, call me. | If you have any questions or need more information about our services, please call me. |

Of course, inserting too much *context* language in a technical document is poor *style*. In fact, as long as *support* and *structure* understand the *statement*, they don't need to know much about *style*; however, *style* needs to know all three. *Style* cannot focus on *support* without knowing the format created by *structure*. Bullets often preclude the use of *context* language, and traditional paragraphs often demand more of it. On the other hand, a failure to use concrete, active verbs in a technical document is also poor *style*. Table 1-8 illustrates this point.

### TABLE 1-8
### CONCRETE AND ACTIVE VERBS

| Avoid Abstract, Passive Directions | Use Concrete, Active Directions |
|---|---|
| The user should perform three actions: <br>• The printer should be functional. <br>• Ascertain that it is stocked with paper. <br>• Depress the icon reading "print." | The user should perform three actions: <br>• Turn on the printer. <br>• Check the paper supply. <br>• Click the print button. |

To see how *statement, support, structure,* and *style* collaborate, imagine that you have to reject Bill Dollar's proposal for renovating your office. A first draft appears in Figure 1-1.

### FIGURE 1-1
### REJECTION LETTER, DRAFT 1

Statement ➡     We must reject your proposal for three reasons.

Support ➡     First, your price quote of $120,000 exceeds our budget by $8,000. Second, your project completion time of 90 days is four weeks longer than we can allow. Third, your offer to do the work only during business hours will be too disruptive to our operations.

Next comes *structure,* which knows that such documents should have a closing as well as an opening and a discussion. It also understands that the *support* should be listed for easy reference. Figure 1-2 shows how *structure* contributes to the document.

## FIGURE 1-2
## REJECTION LETTER, DRAFT 2, ADDING STRUCTURE

Statement ➡ We must reject your proposal for three reasons:

Support ➡
1. Your price quote of $120,000 exceeds our budget by $8,000.

2. Your project completion time of 90 days is four weeks longer than we can allow.

3. Your offer to do the work only during business hours will be disruptive to our operations.

Statement ➡ If you would like to resubmit the proposal, please do so by July 28.

## FIGURE 1-3
## REJECTION LETTER, DRAFT 3, ADDING STYLE

Statement ➡ Thank you for submitting your quote for renovating our offices. We were impressed with the promptness and completeness of your proposal, and we believe that we would benefit from your services. That is why we encourage you to resubmit your proposal with these three points in mind:

Support ➡
1. *Your price quote of $120,000 exceeds our budget by $8,000.* If we purchased Grade B rugs instead of Grade A rugs for the executive suites, would you meet our price? If not, can you suggest other alternatives to control the cost?

2. *Your project completion time of 90 days will encroach on our peak season for four weeks.* Instead of starting the project in May, can you start on April 1? This would give you a June 30 completion date and free our office for the July rush.

3. *Your offer to do the work only during business hours would be disruptive to our operations.* We could endure installation of rugs and cubicle partitions during business hours. But can we compromise by having you install the ceiling tile and new walls after 4:00 p.m.?

Statement ➡ We hope that you will resubmit your proposal by July 28 so that we can decide on the project. Please call me at 732-721-7577 if you have any questions.

Finally, *style* notices that the closing suggests a shift in the *statement* from simply notifying the bidder that the proposal was rejected to inviting the bidder to resubmit a bid. *Style* also realizes that the cold language of the refusal does little to encourage the bidder to participate in future bids.

Figure 1-3 shows how *style* completely reshapes the document to build a relationship with the bidder by adding *context* language to the *content* language.

Technical and scientific writers use *style* as a means of highlighting the subject matter, not for fussing over the personalities involved; nevertheless, they know that *style* helps them connect the subject matter with language in a way that will keep the reader focused.

The writing *product* as seen through the *4S Plan* makes for a useful planning and quality-controlling method because most writers tend to have strengths in some of these areas, and they will use those strengths to improve their weaknesses in the others. For instance, I would encourage purposeful, detailed, and organized writers with tone issues to use their *statement, support,* and *structure* strengths in improving their *style.* Or I would coach writers to use their knowledge of *statement, support,* and *style* when sharpening their *structure.*

Table 1-9 offers some final thoughts on the *4S Plan* to help the writer see the entire writing *product* throughout the writing *process.*

## TABLE 1-9
## THE LIVING 4S PLAN

| Element | Role... | When planning, ask yourself... | When drafting, tell yourself... | When revising, editing, and proofreading, ask yourself... |
|---|---|---|---|---|
| Statement | Manager | What do I want? | Stick to the point! | • Is it clear?<br>• Is it results focused? |
| Support | Worker | What does my reader need to know? | Get it all out! | • Is it complete? |
| Structure | Builder | How should I lay out the information? | Keep it in order! | • Is it organized?<br>• Is it accessible?<br>• Is it consistent? |
| Style | Artist | How should I say it? | Help the reader understand it! | • Is it reader focused?<br>• Is it concise?<br>• Is it courteous?<br>• Is it correct? |

# Tools of the Writer's Trade

Knowing the writing process and the writing product will jumpstart you down the road to on-the-job writing success. But knowledge is useless without action. Chapter 2 will get you started in putting all these ideas to work; however, before showing up to work, you need the tools to get the job done. At the least, you should have the appropriate books, websites, models, word-processing software, notebook, and self-assessment tool.

## Books

Good writers are good readers, but they don't need photographic memories. That's why they keep certain books within an arm's length for reference:

- dictionary
- thesaurus
- writer's handbook

Many are available on-line or in your bookstore.

Many people ask about the value of pocket-sized references. The answer to that question is simple: If it's your back that concerns you, then get the pocket-sized reference; if it's completeness and accuracy that concern you, then get the unabridged reference. These days, the decision is not so simple. Many corporate associates and consultants travel extensively and are unlikely to add such contents to their already heavy baggage. On the other hand, if you write from the office, then the larger references will return your investment many times over. Some writers prefer CD versions of these reference tools; however, most proficient on-the-job writers I have met use both the print and the electronic versions interchangeably—depending on their need for completeness, accuracy, and expediency. Multimedia dictionaries tend to be abridged, lacking the comprehensive etymology and usage notes found in print dictionaries. Yet they are not as unwieldy as desk dictionaries can be; therefore, it's always best to have both so that you can choose as needed.

## Websites

The convenience of the Internet makes access to excellent reference sources a cinch. So many crop up, move, or disappear that you should periodically run searches of words like *writing*, *dictionary*, *thesaurus*, *grammar*, *word usage*, and *punctuation*—and even more specific terms like *run-on sentences*, *active-passive voice*, and *comma usage*—using any of the search engines on the Internet.

Browsing and bookmarking websites will provide you with a writer's library that can give you quick answers to nagging questions about the proper use of *me* or *myself*, placement of apostrophes, or capitalization of uncommon words.

## Models

You should not feel the need to create everything from scratch. Just as we learn to talk by listening to others talk, we could learn good writing by following models. Numerous books available in libraries, bookstores, or online provide hundreds of memo and letter models. Many corporations have massive libraries of standard documents for their employees' use. Keep three points in mind when using model documents:

- Ensure that you have selected a reliable, approved source.
- Determine whether the style of the referenced document suits your purpose (more about that in Chapter 4).
- CARE (**c**hange, **a**dd, **r**eorganize/reformat, and **e**liminate content) as needed so that your writing appears fresh, sincere, and accurate to your readers.

The more effectively you research and adapt excellent models, the more your Level 3 writing (reflective) becomes Level 2 (regulated), which increases your on-the-job writing efficiency.

## Word-Processing Software

Abundant evidence exists to show that word-processing software increases the efficiency and effectiveness of on-the-job writers. Certainly, this software makes revising, editing, saving, and storing easier. Of course, the advantages are counterbalanced by disadvantages. Consider the *Battling I's*, shown in Table 1-10, to avoid the pitfalls posed by your software.

## Notebook

Professional on-the-job writers regularly write in notebooks—of the paper or electronic sort—for many reasons. Here are the three most common reasons that I hear:

- to log activities planned, in progress, or completed
- to take notes at meetings and from reading material or phone conversations

- to brainstorm and organize ideas for projects or documents they're developing

Using a notebook free of any grammatical restriction affects both the *product* and *process*. Writers yield a *product* benefit because by documenting their work and ideas, they have material for their writing tasks. They gain a *process* benefit because the continual writing practice keeps them sharp, making the connection between the brain and the fingers more fluid. These critical ideas get more attention in Chapters 2 and 3.

## TABLE 1-10
## THE BATTLING I'S OF THE INFORMATION AGE

| Element | Positive | Negative |
|---|---|---|
| Integration | Writers can merge voice, data, and images in one package. | Writers spend more time learning new software versions, dealing with glitches, and not using the software to its maximum benefit. |
| Interaction | Writers can engage in two-way communication more frequently and naturally. | Writers produce documents on demand so quickly that they may make sloppy mistakes. |
| Intelligence | Writers have greater capacity, information access, and customizing potential. | Writers spend too much time sifting through useless data pouring into their operating systems. |
| Independence | Writers have freedom to communicate to whomever they want, whenever they want, and about whatever they want. | Writers may overstep their bounds by thoughtlessly sending documents to inappropriate readers. |
| Individuality | Writers have a better opportunity to express themselves more personally, informally, and candidly. | Writers may become too informal and offensive in their style—especially when writing across contrasting cultures. |
| Imagination | Writers have the tools to express themselves to the extent that their creativity allows them. | Writers may overuse multiple font types, styles, and sizes as well as hackneyed phrases and jargon. |

## Self-assessment

Before improving your writing skills, you need to know your strengths and weaknesses in order to set measurable writing goals for yourself and to use your writing strengths in overcoming your writing weaknesses. The *On-the-Job Writing Process/Product Checklist* (page 28) offers you a tool for discovering your strengths and weaknesses. The statements appearing in the Checklist are all positive. Therefore, if you check "always" in response to a prompt, then you can consider that quality a writing strength. Alternatively, if you check "never" or "unsure" in response to a prompt, then you can consider that quality a writing weakness and an area for improvement, and you should learn how to tackle those weaknesses through carefully reading this book and practicing your writing. Note that the qualities are categorized in five domains: process, statement, support, structure, and style.

Once you've completed the checklist, list your goals in the space provided and focus on them as you read this book.

## Summary

Writing is both a process and a product. On-the-job writing success depends on your ability to manage your time (the process) en route to completing a document (the product). Mastering the writing process makes you efficient; mastering the product makes you effective.

The writing process comprises the three PDQ steps: plan, draft, and quality control. When planning, we brainstorm and organize ideas. When drafting, we create a rough copy of those ideas. When quality controlling, we protect our REP: revise the ideas, edit the expression, and proofread a hard copy.

We can assess the writing product by using the 4S Plan: statement, support, structure, and style. The *statement* is the purpose of the document. The *support* is the details supporting the purpose. The *structure* is the organization of the statement and support. The *style* is the balancing of content and context in delivering the statement and support through the structure.

Successful on-the-job writers have within easy reach at all times useful writers' resource books and websites, models of good writing, word-processing software, and a notebook, all of which can help them continually improve the qualities of their writing.

# ON-THE-JOB WRITING
## PROCESS/PRODUCT CHECKLIST

| Scale | 1: Always | 2: Usually | 3: Never | 4: Unsure |
|---|---|---|---|---|

| # | Quality | 1 | 2 | 3 | 4 |
|---|---|---|---|---|---|
| *PROCESS* | | | | | |
| 1 | I am confident in my writing ability. | | | | |
| 2 | I have a procedure for creating documents. | | | | |
| 3 | I write quickly without procrastinating. | | | | |
| 4 | I feel comfortable when writing. | | | | |
| *STATEMENT* | | | | | |
| 5 | Readers easily identify my purpose. | | | | |
| 6 | My documents end with clear next steps. | | | | |
| *SUPPORT* | | | | | |
| 7 | My documents completely support my purpose. | | | | |
| 8 | I answer all my reader's questions, or ask of my reader all I need to know. | | | | |
| *STRUCTURE* | | | | | |
| 9 | I logically arrange the sections of my documents. | | | | |
| 10 | I carefully organize the ideas in my paragraphs. | | | | |
| 11 | I format my documents to increase readability. | | | | |
| 12 | My graphics highlight essential supporting data. | | | | |

| # | Quality | 1 | 2 | 3 | 4 |
|---|---------|---|---|---|---|
| STYLE | | | | | |
| 13 | I balance *content* and *context* language to suit my purpose and the reader's concerns. | | | | |
| 14 | I carefully check for tone problems. | | | | |
| 15 | I present an accurate, unbiased view. | | | | |
| 16 | My sentence structure is clear. | | | | |
| 17 | My sentences are concise. | | | | |
| 18 | I choose concrete, expressive words. | | | | |
| 19 | My writing is free of errors in sentence structure, grammar, diction, punctuation, and mechanics. | | | | |

*My Writing Goals:*

_____

_____

_____

_____

_____

_____

_____

_____

# CHAPTER 2

# Planning

"It is a bad plan that admits of no modifications."

– Publilius Syrus, *Maxim 469*,
1st Century B.C.E.

This chapter describes what you should do to begin challenging work-related documents with an efficient and effective plan. The first step of the PDQ writing process—*planning*—promotes efficiency because it helps you overcome writer's block, enabling you to produce documents quickly. Planning also promotes effectiveness because it helps you generate the necessary ideas that will ultimately appear in your final draft. Chapter 2 is divided into three sections: 1) the reasons for planning documents, 2) an explanation of how the "4S Plan" supports your document planning needs, and 3) a description of the planning techniques.

## Why Plan

No question about it: Writing challenges people—even well-educated people—more than speaking does for at least two reasons:

1. *Writing is not as efficient as speaking.* We speak at a rate of about three or four times faster than we write. That's why we would rather tell or show someone how to perform a procedure than write it down for them.
2. *Feedback is immediate and clear when speaking.* When we speak with someone face to face or over the telephone, our listener immediately responds, ensuring that our information is clear. When writing, we may never receive feedback from our readers, causing possible ambiguity or uncertainty.

Of course, these reasons will not excuse us from writing well. We all need *working papers*, so to speak, to help us recall the details of those important conversations when following up on them. In fact, everything we write on the job is someone else's or our own *management tool*. Imagine your client working through several screens you created from the company help desk; those directions *manage* to get her through a new software application process. Or your manager perusing a proposal that recommends an alteration of the office space; those recommendations *manage* how he will take the next steps related to the proposal. Whatever we write on the job, we write it for a purpose and for a specific audience.

As noted in Chapter 1, we don't want to plan *every* document we write—only those documents that cause us writer's block, that induce procrastination and not inspiration, that riddle us with stress. We plan because we want to eliminate those symptoms and stir our creative juices. And we choose whether to plan a particular document based on purely subjective reasoning. What may challenge me as a writer may not challenge you, but planning the document will jumpstart my thinking through writing. So read through this chapter keeping in mind that it will get you through those moments when you find yourself staring cluelessly at a blank monitor with an approaching deadline, or when you just don't feel inspired to write even a comma, or when your fertile mind is overflowing with ideas and you're too excited to get started coherently.

## Thinking through Writing

Remember the only way to start writing: by writing. This is an important point. You can't get started by simply sitting there and meditating about your topic. You actually have to move your fingers, either by pushing your pen or pencil across a piece of paper to form words, or by tapping at your keyboard to form them on the screen. Anything else is something other than writing.

How often have you heard someone say, or have you said yourself, "I have a hard time getting started, but once I do start I can't stop"? Naturally. You needed to connect the brain to the fingers and think through writing. It's much like the way we speak to one another. When we first meet, some awkward moments may pass. Our speech may be halting, guarded; we may even stumble over a word or two. But once we feel comfortable and connect with each other's language, minutes fly by and we don't bother to censor our speech. Words just burst from our brains and pop from our mouths like an endless barrage of firecrackers without our seeming to think about them.

Yet we are thinking—*thinking through speaking* or *thinking through listening*, depending on which you're doing at the moment. And if you think about it (no pun intended), as you are now—*thinking through reading*—you can think about other things while *thinking through speaking* or *thinking through writing*. Try it during your next informal conversation with friends about, say, food. As you *listen* to your friends speak, think about irrelevant matters, such as Neil Armstrong's moon walk followed by Jennifer Lopez rocking on an electrified stage and see whether you understood what your friends were saying. You probably will. Then as you *speak* to your friend, think about Jack in *The Titanic* sacrificing his life to save Rose from drowning in the North Atlantic Sea, followed by Rev. Martin Luther King, Jr., addressing thousands of people at the Lincoln Memorial, and see whether your friends understood what you were saying. They probably will. As you read this paragraph, were you thinking other thoughts and still understanding these words? I'd bet you were.

A problem for people with writer's block is that they *ponder* instead of *write*—which causes their *writing* minds to go blank. How ironic: They're stressed out because their minds are blank when they unwittingly caused that very effect! Pondering doesn't start until we start to meditate, speaking and listening don't start until we start to speak and listen, reading doesn't start until we start to read, and writing doesn't start until we start to write. So all three steps of the PDQ Process—planning, drafting, quality controlling—require us to write.

## Reasons for Writer's Block

Understanding the PDQ process is so useful because knowing and using it enable you to see the three main causes of writer's block, all of which wreak havoc on your writing productivity. The first cause is a non-process-related one, and the second and third are process-related.

### Reason 1: Internal or external distractions

Distractions may seem too obvious a cause of writer's block to be noteworthy. After all, we all know that if we're pained, tired, or stressed, we cannot work well. But thinking about the factors that cause them forces us to confront some bad writing habits we might have picked up at work and have stuck to our *modus operandi* like a deer tick imbedded in our skin. So first let's look at the examples and then discuss their implications. Distractions may set in from physical, psychological, or environmental sources.

## PHYSICAL SOURCES

- exhausted from working long hours
- drained from performing exceedingly difficult tasks involving a high level of mental acuity and attention
- spent from exerting our bodies during difficult labor such as repeated heavy lifting
- incapacitated by an illness
- intoxicated by alcohol or other mind-altering substances

## PSYCHOLOGICAL SOURCES

- insecure about our writing ability
- distracted by personal crises that transcend workplace issues
- upset with the performance or attitude of teammates, managers, clients, or vendors
- uneasy from the pressure caused by someone's presence as we write

## ENVIRONMENTAL SOURCES

- preoccupied with discomforting environmental matters such as fluctuating or intolerable temperatures, lighting, and noise levels
- bothered by ergonomic issues such as uncomfortable seating, desk arrangement, and writing instrument (e.g., computer, writing pad, pen)

Your control over some of the above problems may be limited. Obviously, if you're tired or distracted by some internal or external problem, your writing productivity will decrease. Pushing yourself to create a document under these conditions is like a quarterback with a broken throwing arm trying to pass his team to victory or an actress with laryngitis trying to sing in a musical. The best solution for any of these physical, psychological, or environmental stressors is to eliminate them, avoid them, or do something else until they pass. This isn't to say that we ever write under ideal conditions; however, the closer we get to them, the more productive we'll be.

### Reason 2: Skipping the planning step

Dashing to the computer to begin writing without a plan will waste time and cause unnecessary stress and procrastination. Imagine a baseball player entering the batter's box without having taken a few swings in the on-deck circle. Or a dancer going onstage without having stretched offstage. In those cases, we're sure to see stiff, labored performances. It's important to remember that writing is as much a physical activity as walking or speaking—and planning is just what we need to warm up to the task.

People often make the mistake of getting started by staring at their blank monitor—a perfect metaphor for their blank thought process at the moment. When you jump ahead to Step 2 by trying to draft and then nothing happens, simply back up to Step 1—planning—and you'll often break the writer's block.

### Reason 3: Doing the drafting and quality-controlling steps simultaneously

Drafting means getting all your thoughts down in sentence form. At this stage, you are not looking for the perfect phrase. Rewriting each sentence until it is the way you want it and then moving on to the next sentence is inefficient. Just get the ideas down; you will be able to revise your ideas, edit your expression, and proofread your hard copy in Step 3. Consider what horror novelist Stephen King advised for writing the first draft in his essay "Everything You Need to Know About Writing Successfully—In Ten Minutes": "Here is your choice: either look it up in the dictionary, thereby making sure you have it right—and breaking your train of thought and the writer's trance in the bargain—or just … correct it later. Why not? Did you think it was going to go somewhere?"

The writing process unites the mind and body to advance our purpose at the service of our readers. In planning, we remove the attitudinal barriers— and to the extent we can, the environmental ones—and we embark on the creative process of composing a document. Our brain is our most precious resource, so we want to tap into its wealth. We do this by conditioning our mind in much the same way that Serena Williams conditions her arms for swinging a racket or Andrea Bocelli conditions his voice for singing.

In her book *How to Write While You Sleep*, author and trainer Elizabeth Irvin Ross offers some interesting suggestions about how conditioning the brain has such significance for writers. Noting that the brain experiences four basic brain wave patterns—*alpha, beta, theta*, and *delta*—she suggests that human creativity peaks when the *alpha* waves are active. *Alpha* waves occur twice daily: when waking up and when falling asleep, moments when we are at our greatest level of relaxation. Therefore, the key to tapping the subconscious mind—that place where our creativity resides—is to condition it by visualization techniques that will spark our imagination throughout the day. By actually suggesting ideas to ourselves when we are most likely to accept them, we start down the road toward realizing those suggestions. Figure 2-1 shows the general pattern in which these brain waves assert themselves in our mind.

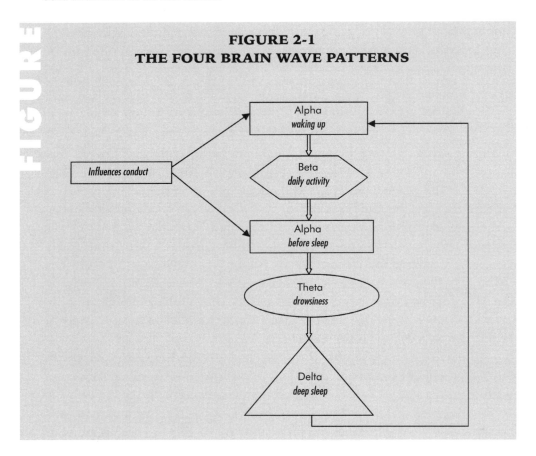

FIGURE 2-1
THE FOUR BRAIN WAVE PATTERNS

So how would visualization during your *alpha* moments actually apply to the sort of writing you do at work: those five pages of meeting minutes you have to get done by tomorrow, or that trip report due next week? Perhaps the first thing to do before sleep is loose any whining about not having the time, energy, or ability to write. Your writing environment at work will not magically alter itself for you. Only you can alter your attitude about that environment. If you can speak your ideas and if you possess basic literacy skills, then you definitely can succeed at writing down your work-related ideas. Creativity isn't as mysterious as most people think. Creativity is not about imagining things that no one else can; it is more about imagining what most people can—if only they *imagined*. What makes on-the-job writing so special is that we always have to imagine our ideas from the reader's perspective.

Next, as you lie in bed, reflect on the assignment you have to write. When relaxing, you can "begin with the end in mind," as corporate consultant Stephen R. Covey puts it. You can imagine the pleasure you'll feel upon completing a results- and reader-focused document. Obviously, you are not literally writing while lying in bed, but you are preparing your mind for the writing task that lies ahead. Since this focused relaxation will spur creative thinking, it is worthwhile to be prepared to write as you lie there. Having a notebook handy for such times can make the difference between a bland and a high-impact message.

What goes into your notebook? Anything that will help you *think through writing* about the assignment ahead. Of course, jumping up in the middle of the night to write an idea—a frequent practice of mine—may do wonders for your writing and do damage to your relationship with anyone lying next to you. Have a penlight nearby too, to respect your significant other's repose!

Another important aspect of tapping into your creative side is allowing serendipity to take over. Not all creative ideas will come to you in a structured sort of way, one that you will immediately recognize in the context of your document. As you are resting, enjoy the discoveries you make and take note of them. Breaking away from your routine way of writing will open you to possibilities you might not have thought existed. Don't forget: sparking your creative side will not make you lose focus. In fact, *willfully imagining* when you're about to take on a challenging writing assignment will in the end help you frame your ideas in the context of your document.

And what exactly is the framework of your document? Regardless of the writing assignment, you will want to consider the 3 A's—the **a**im, the **a**udience, and the **a**rea—to jumpstart the writing process. The following section will show you how to plan your documents—brainstorm and organize your ideas—with the 3 A's.

## What to Plan For

As soon as you begin your document, write down the 3 A's—**a**im, **a**udience, **a**rea—to cover all the issues related to your purpose and your reader's needs. Ask yourself the following questions:

AIM
- What do I want?
- Why do I want it?
- Who besides me wants it?
- When do I want it?
- Where do I want it?
- How do I want it?

AUDIENCE
- Who are my primary readers?
- Who are my secondary readers?

AREA
- What do my primary readers need to know?
- What questions might the secondary readers have?
- In what order would the questions arise?

Let's take the aim, audience, and area one at a time.

## Aim

The aim, or purpose statement, is the mission statement of the document. A clear aim will guide the reader through the content that follows; the absence of a clear aim will puzzle, bore, or even infuriate a reader. Why write anything at work if we're not sure why we're writing it? Purposeful writers keep their aim—what they want their documents to achieve—in front of them at all times.

How do you keep your aim in front of you? Not by simply meditating on it, but by writing it down. Again, this is writing, not meditating. You can try to create your aim by following either of the methods below:

Method 1: Complete the sentence "The aim of this document is to...."

Method 2: Complete the sentence "As a result of reading my document, my reader will...."

This seems deceptively easy, but it demands careful and clear expression. Too often, people will write their aim as

Aim 1: "The aim of this document is to improve our working environment" or

> Aim 2: "As a result of reading my document, my reader will agree that hiring an additional staff person will help our team."

Both of these aims are weak because they do not go far enough toward achieving the writer's intended results.

The first one lacks the accuracy needed of purposeful writing. The writer says that the document aims to "improve the working environment"; however, documents are nothing more than words on paper. *Documents don't improve anything; people do.* Missing in this aim are the specific actions expected of the reader. With this important point in mind, the writer tries again: "The aim of this document is for my manager to reassign office space." Now the action expected of the reader is clear. At this point, you may be protesting, "But I wouldn't dare direct my manager in writing to reassign office space!" Agreed. But you're jumping the gun. We'll deal with *how* we say it when we consider the second A—*audience*. Nevertheless, we still have to make clear the request for reassigning office space. To understand what I mean, imagine that Charlie wants to propose marriage to Maggie. He's quite shy and lacking confidence to begin with, and he has committed a flaw fatal to his proposal: he didn't practice saying precisely what he wanted to say so that Maggie would listen. They meet at a moonlit lake one summer evening, and here is how the conversation goes:

| | |
|---|---|
| Charlie: | Maggie, I … uh … have something important to tell you. |
| Maggie: | What is it, Charlie? |
| Charlie: | I, uh … You … |
| Maggie: | Yes? |
| Charlie: | You … uh … look pretty tonight. |
| Maggie: | Thank you. |
| Charlie: | Yeah. Your … uh … hair so nicely reflects the moonlight. |
| Maggie: | Awww! |
| Charlie: | Yeah. Uh … and your dress, it's … I don't know. |
| Maggie: | It's what? |
| Charlie: | It fits you perfectly. |
| Maggie: | That's so sweet of you. |

| | |
|---|---|
| Charlie: | I know. I mean … uh … |
| Maggie: | Is that what you wanted to tell me? |
| Charlie: | No. I mean, yeah. Of course I want to tell you that. It's true. It's just that … |
| Maggie: | *(Concerned:)* What? |
| Charlie: | That's not important. |
| Maggie: | *(Hurt:)* It's not? |
| Charlie: | I mean, it's important, but not the important thing I wanted to say. |
| Maggie: | I don't get it, Charlie. First you say you just wanted to say that I look beautiful. Then you say it's true. Then you say it's unimportant. Then you say you wanted to say something more important. But you haven't said it. Are you saying that everything you've said is unimportant? Then why are you saying it? |
| Charlie: | Well, if you give me a chance … |
| Maggie: | Give you a chance? I'm afraid that's all I've been doing tonight. |
| Charlie: | Now wait a minute. |
| Maggie: | Okay. Go ahead. I'm all ears, pal. Just what have you got to say that's so important to you, Charlie? Huh? |
| Charlie: | Forget it now. |
| Maggie: | Why should I? |
| Charlie: | You broke the mood. |
| Maggie: | What mood? This you-look-so-pretty-just-kidding-blah-blah-blah smokescreen. *That* mood. Puleeeze. |
| Charlie: | If you'd just let me talk … |
| Maggie: | Why should I? I "broke the mood." Ewww. |

Poor Charlie. Not that I blame Maggie. She reminds me of the office manager who has just heard a staff person complain about office space problems when the staff person really had a great idea for reconfiguring space—but never said it. All the staff person did was whine, whine, whine. And that's all that the office manager heard. The staff person never got around to saying, "I have a great idea to solve some of the office space problems we've been dealing with." If you don't say it, your listener doesn't hear it; likewise, if you don't write it, you reader doesn't read it.

The second aim above comes closer than the first to an intended result, but it still misses the mark. Here the writer wants the reader "to agree" with her opinion on hiring additional staff. Literally, the reader can respond to her memo by saying, "I agree with your point. Thank you." Is agreement what the writer wanted? Of course, but agreement doesn't go far enough. She wants her manager to do something as a result of reading her proposal. Thus, she changes her aim to

> "As a result of reading my document, my manager will hire an additional staff person to help our team."

Is this a bold statement? Yes. But is it what the writer really wants? Absolutely.

Notice in both cases what happened to the writers' sentences from a grammatical perspective: The verbs changed. The first aim changed from "improve" to "reassign"; the second from "agree" to "hire." In purposeful and crisp writing, the verbs anchor each sentence, locking the readers into the writer's vision, steering them toward a clear action, toward what the writer wants. (I'll talk more about verbs in Chapters 4 and 5.)

Clear, crisp writing raises another legitimate concern for the writer. How aggressive should an aim be? After all, in the two examples above, don't the writers seem pushy with their managers? These questions are excellent responses to the forceful nature of purposeful writing. They suggest sensitivity to the reader's concerns. We'll deal with this matter fully in the next section about audience. Before moving on, however, you'll want to think beyond "what do I want" by answering the questions: When do I want it? Why do I want it? Who besides me wants it? Where do I want it? How do I want it? In the examples above, the writers would not want to give their managers ultimatums, but they would want an answer to the question "when do I want it" for three reasons:

1. *Writers who know when they want something will better determine how to manage the required writing time.* For instance, assume Barbara needs a widget in two days. She needs a day to write the proposal to her manager, and her manager needs two days to respond. Barbara has choices to make. If the process takes three days but she wants results in two, is writing the best way to

achieve her goal? Wouldn't a brief meeting with the manager be a better idea? Another choice she needs to make is whether she really needs her request fulfilled in two days.

2. *Writers who know when they want something will better help their readers manage their time.* Thinking about when she wants her request fulfilled increases her sensitivity toward the readers' needs. She will likely set more realistic deadlines for readers' actions.

3. *Writers who know when they want something will think about whether they can contribute to the results they want.* Instead of closing her document with the overused and often inaccurate "Call me if you have questions," Barbara may now think about how she can help her reader do what she expects. She may now close with "With your approval, I will design the office reorganization plan" or "I will be pleased to begin the candidate selection process at your request." (More about purposeful closings in Chapter 4.)

You can figure out on your own why considering the other matters—why I want it, who besides me wants it, where I want it, and how do I want it—would sharpen your aim. Two final points about the aim:

1. *Every standard document needs an aim.* If the document is simply a set of instructions for the XYZ machine, then the aim may be "to guide the reader in safely and efficiently using and maintaining the XYZ machine." If the document is the Project A Team's meeting minutes, then the aim may be "to note the minutes of the Project A Team meeting of May 7." If the document is a letter of resignation, then the aim may be "to state my resignation from Company C effective May 9." The aim is always necessary in guiding writers through the writing process and achieving their intended results.

2. *Every document needs only one aim.* Often people say that they have two aims. This actually should never be the case. Someone may say, "I want my manager to hire an additional staff person, and I want to improve the working environment." The fact is that the first statement is the aim of the document, and the second is a possible result of the aim. The first answers the question, "What do I want?" and the second answers "What

will getting what I want achieve?" Stating a singular aim keeps the writer on track throughout the rest of the planning step.

## Audience

Let's begin this discussion about audience by saying again that documents cannot achieve things, but people can. Armed with that knowledge, you'll want to ensure that your aim is as clear as possible to your audience. If you proposed an idea to your manager, teammates, or clients, your document cannot *make* them accept your idea—*only they can make themselves accept your idea*. With that in mind, you will want to be sure that you address every issue the readers may have about your document.

Understanding your audience goes hand in hand with knowing your aim. In Chapter 1, we talked about the *primary* reader and the *secondary* reader. Let's revisit those distinctions:

- The *primary* readers are the persons to whom you address the message.
- The *secondary* readers are, in short, others who may pick up the document for any number of reasons.

Here's an example of why the writer should consider both the primary and secondary readers. Patricia, an engineer, must write an e-mail to Tom, a product designer, reminding him of next week's quality control meeting. She thinks that since Tom has attended many of these quality control meetings, he would need only the answers to basic questions about the meeting, such as:

- the specific date and time (Monday, June 20, at 10:00 a.m.)
- the place (604 Jefferson Street, fourth floor conference room)
- the purpose of the meeting (to design and deploy a new QC form for manufacturing Model 123)
- the expected attendees (Carl, Production Manager; Sally, Quality Assurance Director; Jeanne, Model 123 Section Supervisor; and Tom and Patricia)
- the agenda items (designing the QC form, developing a training session for using the form, scheduling the deployment of the form)

Figure 2-2 shows how that e-mail might look. (The aim, or purpose statement, is highlighted for illustrative purposes only.)

## FIGURE 2-2
## REMINDER E-MAIL, FIRST DRAFT

To:    Tom Pastoris
From:  Patricia Reynolds
Re:    Next QC Meeting
Date:  June 13, 2005

Tom,

Here is the reminder of next week's Quality Control meeting.

| | |
|---|---|
| **Date:** | Monday, June 20, 2005 |
| **Time:** | 10:00 a.m.–11:30 a.m. |
| **Site:** | 604 Jefferson Street, 4th floor conference room |
| **Purpose:** | To design and deploy a new QC form for manufacturing Model 123 |
| **Invited:** | Carl Schwartz, Production Manager; Sally Perkins, Quality Assurance Director; Jeanne Magliore, Model 123 Section Supervisor, Tom Pastoris, Engineer I; Patricia Reynolds, Product Designer |
| **Agenda:** | · Designing the QC form |
| | · Developing a training session for using the form |
| | · Scheduling the deployment of the form |

I'll see you Monday.

Patricia

However, Patricia is not sure whether Tom or his assistant Jacqueline will attend. If Tom attends, he needs nothing more than the bullet points noted on the list; if Jacqueline attends, she would benefit from knowing at least the following points:

- what her role will be at the meeting
- what the current QC form looks like
- who uses the form
- what the new form should have that the current form doesn't have
- how she can contact Patricia if she has a question

Also, Patricia realizes that Vanessa, Vice-president of Operations, has high expectations of the Quality Control Group, but Vanessa's engagement in other administrative activities precludes her from attending the group's meetings. Patricia needs to keep Vanessa informed about the group's progress in streamlining operations while maintaining high quality standards. Therefore, she decides that she will forward a copy of the e-mail to Vanessa and add one sentence about why the current form needs revision.

## FIGURE 2-3
## REMINDER E-MAIL, SECOND DRAFT

To:     Tom Pastoris
From:   Patricia Reynolds
Re:     Next QC Meeting
Date:   June 13, 2005
Copy:   Vanessa Del Toro

Tom,

*As you know, we discussed at our last Quality Control meeting the need to revise the Model 123 QC form so that it is more comprehensive, flexible, and user friendly for our operators. Therefore, the revision of the form will be the focus of the Quality Control Group's next meeting.* Below are the details to help you prepare for the meeting.

**Date:**    Monday, June 20, 2005
**Time:**    10:00 a.m.–11:30 a.m.
**Site:**    604 Jefferson Street, 4th floor conference room
**Purpose:** To design and deploy a new QC form for manufacturing Model 123
**Invited:** Carl Schwartz, Production Manager; Sally Perkins, Quality Assurance Director; Jeanne Magliore, Model 123 Section Supervisor; Tom Pastoris, Engineer I; Patricia Reynolds, Product Designer

| **Agenda:** | Topic | Owners |
|---|---|---|
| | Designing the QC form | *Jeanne, Tom, Patricia* |
| | Developing a training session for using the form | *Carl, Jeanne, Sally* |
| | Scheduling the deployment of the form | *Carl, Sally* |

*If you need a copy of the current form or need more information to prepare for the meeting, please call me at 579-6420 X138.* I'll see you Monday unless I hear otherwise.

Patricia

Figure 2-3 shows how Patricia adds *context* language to support the needs of her secondary readers. This addition of *context* language emerges from the situation of the document and the relationship of the writer to the reader. Notice how the additional context makes the purpose statement seem more supportive. Patricia is still writing a reminder about the meeting. (The new *context* language is italicized, and the restated aim is highlighted for illustrative purposes only.)

In Figure 2-3, we clearly see how the *style* has changed. The sentences in the opening and closing paragraphs of Draft 2 seem more formal than in Draft 1. This is because Patricia's audience has expanded. Most times, the wider the audience, the more formal the style; therefore, *context* determines *content* as much as the *content* determines *context*. All too often, people begin writing under the assumption that their readers understand the *context* and the *content* of the document; as a result, they fail to hit the right notes for secondary readers who may need the document. In such cases, even if the primary readers understand the message the first time they read it, they might have difficulty understanding it when they pick it up for a different reason several days or weeks later. Professional on-the-job writers know the importance of reaching both their primary and the secondary readers.

## Area

Once you know the *aim* and *audience* of your document, you should have an easy time determining its *area*, the last of the 3 A's in the planning step. The *area*, also known as the scope or supporting details of the document, addresses the key issues the *audience* may consider about the writer's *aim*. Figure 2-4 represents Patricia's notes to herself before writing the e-mail to Tom. It shows how Patricia answers specific questions that Tom, Jacqueline, Vanessa, or any member of the Quality Control group might have. Look back to Figure 2-3 and see where Patricia answers the questions in Figure 2-4.

Of course, every document requires a different aim, audience, and area. The area becomes particularly tricky when jumping from memos of request to formal client proposals to company-wide policy directives. The critical thing to remember is that being clear on what you want (the aim) and from whom you want it (the audience) will guide you in determining your area. Also, notice how in Figure 2-4, the 4S Plan—*statement, support, structure,* and *style*—appears as an uncredited helper:

· Statement: the *Aim*

- Support:  the *Area* questions
- Structure:  the ordering of the *Area* questions
- Style:  consideration of the *Audience* (more about this later in the chapter when we consider the *Audience Survey*).

FIGURE

## FIGURE 2-4
## THE 3A WORKSHEET—AIM, AUDIENCE, AREA

Aim:          To inform about the next meeting
Audience:     Tom, Jacqueline, Vanessa, Carl, Sally, Jeanne
Area:
- When is the meeting?
- Where is the meeting?
- Who are attending?
- What is the purpose of the meeting?
- When did we raise this issue previously?
- Why should we devote an entire meeting to the QC form?
- Who will use the QC form?
- What is the meeting's agenda?
- Who is responsible for each part of the meeting?
- Where can you get additional information?

We'll see other situations as we move along in this chapter and in Chapters 3 and 4. For now, with the aim, audience, and area firmly in mind, let's discuss some planning techniques before writing a draft.

## How to Plan

When planning, you complete two tasks:

- *Brainstorm* ideas about your purpose, readers, supporting details, and next steps by writing them down as they occur to you
- *Organize* the ideas into a workable outline by ordering them in a way that makes sense to your reader and purpose. You also may be adding or deleting information.

How you plan any job-related document depends entirely on your own preferences, the complexity of the document, and the time you have to complete it. Do whatever it takes to get the ideas flowing. You may want to use *boilerplate, planning templates, audience surveys, idea lists, idea tags,* or *idea maps,* to mention six techniques. Each offers powerful advantages in stimulating creativity, so decide which ones you'd be inclined to try.

# Technique 1: Boilerplate

The use of boilerplate, or standardized text, is a good way to turn a blank screen or page into an instant document from which you can select the appropriate language for your purpose and audience. The danger here is becoming too dependent on formulaic writing that becomes hackneyed and turns off your readers. For instance, if the dull and inexact "As per your request, attached are the QXZ specifications" gets your writing going, then use it in first draft; however, remember that when you edit the draft, you should change the phrase to something more meaningful and accurate, such as "I have attached the QXZ specifications you requested at our last Quality Control Committee meeting."

Using boilerplate is a way of processing words by both reading and writing. You don't want to mindlessly use the same text you used last time if it doesn't fit the occasion this time. Still, you may want to read previously written documents on your topic until an idea pops into your head that starts the writing. This practice is no different from how most of us wrote during our school days: we read a poem, then we wrote a poem; we read a descriptive essay, then we wrote a descriptive essay; we read a critique of a novel, then we wrote a critique of the critique.

How would this work on the job? For instance, your manager assigns you to write the minutes for the Quality Control Committee's next weekly meeting. After the meeting, you return to your office armed with a slew of notes, and you aren't sure about what to include in the minutes. So you pick up a copy of the last meeting minutes, which you know the committee accepted with no amendments. You begin to read them and come across a topic that you covered at the meeting. Paraphrasing from this section of the minutes, you are now ready to dive into the writing assignment. Reading is often a great way to jumpstart the writing process.

# Technique 2: Planning Templates

Using a planning template is another way of turning a blank screen or page into instant text. The planning template is like the *3A Worksheet* in Figure 2-4, except that it is more customized to the document type. You can make one for internal proposals, agendas, operating procedures, company newsletter articles—any document type. The more you make, the more prepared you are to immediately start writing on demand. Figure 2-5 shows a planning template model for an internal proposal. Note that the *next steps*, which

## FIGURE 2-5
## SAMPLE PLANNING TEMPLATE

| Internal Proposal | | |
|---|---|---|
| **Aim** | *Purpose:* | Propose weekly meeting with Information Technology Team |
| | *Next Steps:* | 1.  I'll create an IT checklist |
| | | 2.  Set up meeting with Jason Jeffers to plan first meeting |
| **Audience** | *Primary:* | Myra Schreiber, Manager |
| | *Secondary:* | •  Jason Jeffers, Manager, Information Technology Team |
| | | •  Members of my group |
| **Area** | *Problem:* | Our server has crashed three times in the past month. |
| | *Impact:* | We can't make the necessary changes to our website in a timely manner. Our clients are complaining about receiving outdated information, and our web designers are idle for long periods. |
| | *Background:* | Since the recent acquisition of the Frost Group's IT team, our IT service has worsened. |
| | *Solutions:* | Create IT Checklist and propose weekly status meeting to cover: |
| | | •  troubleshooting reports |
| | | •  planned server updates |
| | *Benefits:* | To Us |
| | | 1.  We'll be more reliable and prompt in responding to our clients' requests for information. |
| | | 2.  We'll have less downtime. |
| | | 3.  We'll develop stronger ties to IT. |
| | | To IT |
| | | 1.  They'll have a better reputation for client service. |
| | | 2.  They'll free up a lot of their troubleshooting time through good planning. |

would appear at the end of the final draft, appear under *Aim* in the planning template. I do this to remember the close connection between establishing a clear purpose statement and following through with purposeful next steps.

Remember two important points about the planning template in Figure 2-5, one having to do with the writing process and the other with the writing product. First, chances are that the writer in the example wouldn't need to plan as much as the table shows. Perhaps a sentence or two would get him cranked up and ready to fire words into his first draft. But if he runs out of ideas and gets stuck midway through the draft, he would return to the planning template. Second, don't let the neatness of the illustration fool you. The planning template is a writer's tool to be seen by his or her eyes only. Neatness and orderliness don't matter—all that does is the writer's success at generating ideas and overcoming writer's block.

## Technique 3: Audience Surveys

The *audience survey* is also a highly individualized tool for planning complex documents. It is a good way to get into your readers' minds. I compare it to what someone may do before buying a gift for someone she cares about. She'd put aside her own preferences to think about what she could buy to make her loved one happy. Her purpose? To let him know that she cares about him. Her vehicle? The shirt. Or watch. Or CD. Or flowers. Whatever she thinks would most touch him. Audience surveys are like this. The writer gives his reader the gift of his document. His purpose: To let her know how to operate the X7 software program. His vehicle? Whatever information he thinks she would need to operate the program. He has to set aside his own perspective as a subject-matter expert to think about what she may and may not know about the program. He has to answer each question she may have— and answer it with language that she can understand.

The audience survey goes far beyond the *who, what, when, where, why,* and *how* of the document. Those six words are helpful for some writing situations; however, they're too general and often don't get to the heart of the writer's purpose and the audience's needs. Answering specific questions that you think your readers might have heightens the power of your communication—giving you a presence with your readers as they read your document.

To make the audience survey work for most on-the-job writing situations, create a list of questions that cover the range of your writing assignments. This way, you won't have to make a new audience survey for each document. Experience will help you modify questions on your list. Figure 2-6 shows a possible audience survey that you can use to get started. Remember: You will not always have to answer *every* question for *every* situation you write about—just those that relate to your readers.

**FIGURE 2-6**
## SAMPLE AUDIENCE SURVEY

What do I want to give or get from my reader?
>   To get Monica's approval in hiring a summer intern for the new-hire orientation
>   program

Who is/are my primary reader(s)?
>   Monica (my manager)

Who is/are my secondary reader(s)?
>   · Christine Ross (Vice-president, Monica's manager)
>   · Jillian Weinstein (my teammate)
>   · Carlos Leandre (Director, Human Resources)

What do my readers need to know about my purpose?
>   · *Why we need an intern for the summer*
>       1. inadequate coverage because of summer vacations
>       2. increased responsibilities because of the new-hire orientation program
>   · *Why we have inadequate coverage*
>       Four of the five people in our group will vacation at different times in July
>       and August
>   · *How responsibilities have increased*
>       Human Resources has asked us to provide training material for the
>       orientation program
>   · *What the intern will do*
>       1. type training manuals
>       2. photocopy materials
>       3. research training resources on the Internet
>       4. distribute materials
>       5. create a new associate database
>       6. provide phone coverage
>   · *Who the intern's supervisor will be*
>       Jillian Weinstein
>   · *What we will have to pay the intern*
>       Human Resources currently pays a summer intern $15 per hour
>   · *What the intern's duration of employment will be*
>       May 29 – August 17
>   · *When the hiring process should begin*
>       April 16
>   · *What the deadline is for creating the position*
>       March 30

Does my reader have the authority to implement my request?
>   No. She needs approval from Christine Ross.

How can I show my readers the importance of this issue?
>   · We want to impress the new hires with an efficient orientation process
>   · We want to open communication with the placement office of local universities

Again, notice how the 4S Plan comes into play with the audience survey, especially the most challenging S, *style*:

· **S**tatement: *What do I want to give or get from my reader?*
· **S**upport: *What do my readers need to know about my purpose?*
· **S**tructure: *How do I organize the support?* (In Figure 2-6, this question is not explicitly shown, but it is answered through the organization of the questions and answers.)
· **S**tyle: *Who is/are my primary reader(s)? Who is/are my secondary reader(s)? Does my reader have the authority to implement my request? How can I show my readers the importance of this issue?*

The last two questions in style serve a critical purpose: They move the writer from thinking about what she wants (purpose) to what her readers want (audience). Now she begins to think of questions her readers might have, and she tries to see the situation not only from her and her teammates' little corner of the company but from the broader perspectives of her manager, her manager's manager, and the human resources division. This thinking sets her on her way to writing like a manager.

## Technique 4: Idea Lists

The idea list is perhaps the easiest planning technique. When creating an idea list, you are not writing sentences but brief phrases or single words—even pictures—to capture all the necessary ideas for your document. Remember that in planning, *brainstorming* comes before *organizing*, so you should list all your ideas before changing them. Start with a blank page or screen and complete the following five steps:

1. *State your aim (purpose)*. This statement need not be a formal sentence, just a written reminder that you have in front of you for reference when completing the idea list.
2. *List every idea about the aim that comes to your mind*. Don't worry about writing down something foolish; no one but you is looking at your idea list.
3. *Organize ideas in groups with "working titles" using a logical order*. Here you transition from brainstorming to organizing. Start with your purpose statement and imagine yourself in a dialogue with the reader. This practice will help you determine the best order for the ideas. Even if in your finished draft you never use the working titles (e.g., advantages, disadvantages,

costs, benefits, problem, history, conclusions, recommendations), using them during planning and drafting will help you control your ultimate organization.

4. *Delete ideas that don't fit.* As you organize your list and group your ideas with working titles, you'll find that some ideas you brainstormed don't belong in your document. Just rub them out.

5. *Add ideas as they occur to you.* Organizing and grouping your list will expose holes in your development. If ideas that can plug the holes pop into your head, write them down and place them where they belong.

In the example below, Claudia, a pharmaceutical salesperson, uses an idea list to kick off the writing process for a document persuading her manager Kenny and the chief financial officer Wendy to buy a handheld computer for each member of her group.

*Step 1: State your aim (purpose)*
Get Kenny's approval to purchase seven HandyDandy Ix handhelds for our group.

*Step 2: List every idea about the aim that comes to your mind.*

| | | |
|---|---|---|
| Cost | Discount | Downloading |
| Great features | Weight | Synchronizing |
| Usability | User ease | Technical support |
| Business needs | Phone | Power |
| Size | Pager | Software interfacing |
| Dependability | Endorsements | Calculator |
| Durability | Storage capability | Visit website |

*Step 3: Organize ideas in groups with "working titles" using a logical order.* (Note: the boldface words are the "working titles," and the group at the end with a question mark did not fit anywhere.)

| **Opening** | **Convenience** | **Versatility** | **Next Steps** |
|---|---|---|---|
| Business needs | Size | Storage capability | Visit website |
| Great features | Weight | Software interfacing | |
| | Synchronizing | Downloading | **?** |
| **Popularity** | Power | Phone | Usability |
| Endorsements | Technical support | Pager | User ease |
| | | Calculator | Dependability |
| | **Affordability** | | Durability |
| | Cost | | |
| | Discount | | |

*Step 4: Delete ideas that don't fit.*

Claudia deletes the items under the question mark for different reasons:

- Usability—too general a word, which she will cover under the group **versatility**
- User ease—a repetition of the group **convenience**
- Dependability—just doesn't fit into the ideas she wants to convey
- Durability—a repetition of the item *power* in the group **convenience**

*Step 5: Add ideas as they occur to you.*

Claudia sees some holes in her organization and she plugs them with additional ideas. (They appear in italics).

**Opening**
Business needs: *better organization, handling information overload*
Great features *to make us more organized and efficient*

**Popularity**
Endorsements *from national trade magazines*
Endorsements *from our clients*
Endorsements *from our vendors*
Endorsements *from other groups in our company*

**Versatility**
Storage capability
Software interfacing
*Organizing to-do's, date book, memos, e-mail*
Downloading
Phone
Pager
*Tape recorder*
Calculator

**Convenience**
Size
Weight
Synchronizing
*Sharing: Beam-Me-In technology*
Power
Technical support

**Affordability**
Cost
Discount

**Next Steps**
*HandyDandy sales rep available for a demo*
Visit website
*I can begin the requisitioning process*

With this document plan in hand, Claudia should be ready to write her first draft of the proposal.

# Technique 5: Idea Tags

Using idea tags to get the writing process started is similar to using idea lists. Start *brainstorming* by randomly listing ideas related to your purpose on index cards or post-its (one idea per tag) on a large, blank sheet of paper. As with all the planning activities, you need not write sentences; single words or brief phrases will do. If you're itching to write sentences, then you're not planning—you're drafting. This desire to draft is fine; go with it. Just beware that drafting might make you lose some critical ideas that you would have captured more easily by using a planning technique. If you sense this happening, just go back to the planning step.

After you have run out of ideas, start *organizing* by arranging the ideas in a sensible order relevant to your reader, deleting irrelevant ideas and adding useful ones on new tags as you go along. Finally, read the assembled idea tags from top to bottom, ensuring that all your ideas connect logically to your purpose and your reader's concerns.

Figure 2-7 illustrates how idea tags would work for Pedro, an investment banker, planning a memo to Noreen, his website management contractor, about suggested changes to the division's website. First he *brainstorms*.

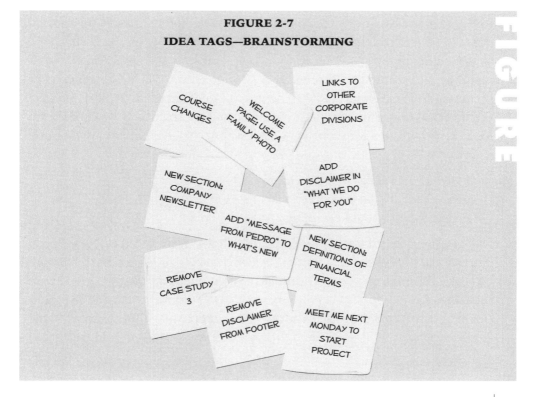

**FIGURE 2-7**

**IDEA TAGS—BRAINSTORMING**

Next, he organizes, rearranging, deleting, and adding idea tags, as shown in Figure 2-8. (Note: Underlining indicates an added idea tag, and boldface indicates a deleted idea tag.) Notice that Pedro doesn't bother grouping ideas by using explicit working titles, as called for in idea lists. Of course, he can add working titles if he wants to, but he feels that this would be overdoing it since he already has a good idea of how he wants to organize his points.

Also notice how he actually did create an order for his ideas and grouped them by line:

- His first line states his purpose.
- His second line notes the item for removal.
- His third and fourth lines describe items for addition to individual pages.
- His fifth line indicates new sections for addition to the website.
- His sixth line shows new links from the website.
- His seventh line follows through on his purpose.

Pedro should now be ready to write a first draft of his document.

## Technique 6: Idea Maps

If idea tags and especially idea lists feel too linear and restrictive for you, try the idea map, which is the technique I turn to when I am most baffled by a writing assignment: Am I writing a complaint or a request? Am I recommending a two-step or a three-step course of action? Have I considered all the possible causes for a plant accident or for declining sales? Should I reject the proposal outright or suggest modifications to it? I find it especially useful as a springboard into writing a draft whenever I feel uncertain about:

- my purpose
- what my reader needs to know
- my reader's possible response
- the tone I should establish

Idea maps are like mind mapping, which was introduced by Tony Buzan in *The Mind Map Book: How to Use Radiant Thinking to Maximize Your Brain's Untapped Potential*, as a way of stimulating creativity. Among its premises are the ideas that (1) our visual memory works astoundingly well, and (2) traditional note taking discourages the needed skill of connecting concepts to the key words associated with them. In my experience of using mind mapping

# FIGURE 2-8
## IDEA TAGS—ORGANIZING

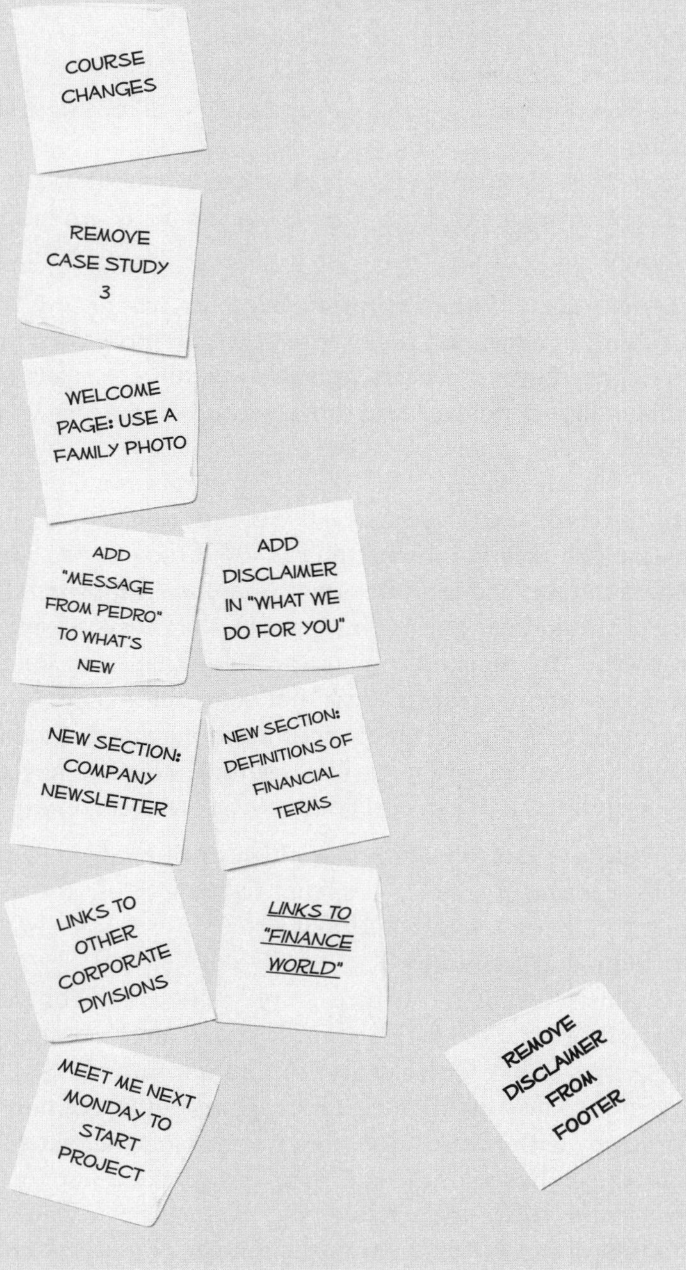

COURSE CHANGES

REMOVE CASE STUDY 3

WELCOME PAGE: USE A FAMILY PHOTO

ADD "MESSAGE FROM PEDRO" TO WHAT'S NEW

ADD DISCLAIMER IN "WHAT WE DO FOR YOU"

NEW SECTION: COMPANY NEWSLETTER

NEW SECTION: DEFINITIONS OF FINANCIAL TERMS

LINKS TO OTHER CORPORATE DIVISIONS

LINKS TO "FINANCE WORLD"

MEET ME NEXT MONDAY TO START PROJECT

REMOVE DISCLAIMER FROM FOOTER

and observing numerous clients use it, I have noticed many benefits, the five most valuable being that writers:

- approach the writing task with greater confidence
- draft the document with greater ease
- maintain continuity with their central point
- provide more relevant details for their readers
- create a positive tone so vital to the reader's accepting their viewpoint

To map your ideas for a topic, you will not need a computer; all you need are a group of contrasting-color pens or pencils and a blank, unlined sheet of paper. Then follow these steps:

1. *Draw in the center of the page a picture symbolizing your topic.* If you cannot think of a symbol, then write down no more than one or two words; however, keep in mind that pictures are easier to remember than words. You do not have to be an artist to do this. Remember: Only you will see your idea map.
2. *Using different colors, draw branches from the central symbol, connecting them to key pictures or words.* The use of different colors helps emphasize your key points, highlights the direction you want your ideas to take, and reinforces your memory. Important: Do not use any judgment during this step. Include every idea that occurs to you and suspend your "critical thinking." These first two steps are about creating ideas, not controlling them.
3. *Number the ideas that you'll use to support your purpose and address your readers' concerns.* Here you shift from *brainstorming* to *organizing*—ordering, deleting, and adding ideas as necessary.

That's it. Really. It doesn't seem like much until you've tried it a few times, but it is a powerful tool for breaking writer's block and any stress related to the topic. It also makes for a great strategic tool when brainstorming during problem-solving sessions.

Figure 2-9 illustrates an excellent example of how someone can overcome any negativity associated with a topic. It shows an idea map by Gina, a 23-year-old college graduate with a degree in communications. She has been working one year for Know-It-All, Inc., a prestigious public opinion research firm. She is unhappy with her position because she feels that she hasn't had the opportunities she deserves. This feeling has plagued her for the past month and has made her consider requesting a transfer. She wants to write her manager a memo requesting the transfer, but she does not want to come

# FIGURE 2-9
## MIND MAPPING

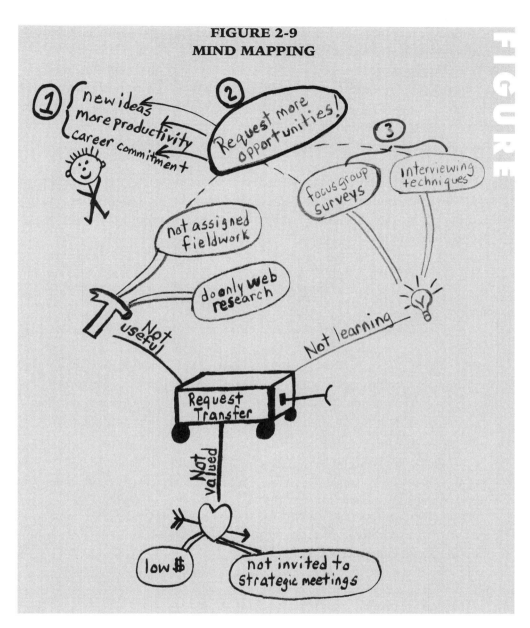

across as a complainer. After all, she likes her manager, even though she feels that he has overlooked her talent. Furthermore, she knows that her potential manager will read the memo, so she does not want to start off on the wrong foot by seeming like a malcontent. Finally, she is aware that language such as "underused" and "undervalued" creates a negative tone that she wants to avoid.

Many interesting moments occur as Gina creates her idea map. Here are five memorable ones:

1. *She gets started immediately.* She starts with a central point of "request transfer," which she knows her manager may take as a sign of discontent. But she plays with the idea map knowing full well that she needs a better reason to write—though at first she can't think of one. Rather than waste time by letting herself stew about her dilemma, she begins the creative process with the negative thought.

2. *She becomes playful about the situation.* Notice the picture she chooses to symbolize her request for a transfer: a child's wagon. She knows she may be coming across like a pouting kindergartner threatening to run away from home. Even the pictures symbolizing her three reasons for the request (the heart for "not valued," the hammer for "not useful," and the light bulb for "not learning") are equally playful. Do not mistake this practice as an attempt at self-mockery. Gina is just tapping into her *brain* and distancing herself from her *heart*; she's thinking, not emoting.

3. *She is quick to abandon dead ends.* Once she comes up with two reasons for her Not Valued section, she realizes she is raising issues that may appear irrelevant. For one, she may be unhappy with her low salary, but she might not know for sure that her salary is not equal to other new associates in her group. She also realizes that her manager's not inviting her to strategic meetings can be an honest, unintentional oversight rather than a calculated decision to exclude her.

4. *She is quick at making connections between needs and wants.* Once she writes down "not assigned fieldwork" in her Not Useful section, and "focus group surveys" and "interviewing techniques" in her Not Learning section, she realizes that she has never asked for these opportunities. This realization leads her to a new idea—that she should request opportunities before complaining about not having them.

5. *She is quick to abandon her negative central idea in favor of a positive one.* She now changes her central idea from requesting a transfer to requesting more opportunities within her group. She sees three reasons to make her manager see the situation as she does, as shown on the upper left of the idea map: she can contribute new ideas to the group, increase her personal productivity, and fully commit herself to the organization. She scraps everything on her idea map that does not point to the idea "request more opportunities" because she no longer needs it. This is not to say that she wasted her time with useless ideas. Without plotting her ideas as they occurred to

her, she would not have arrived at her new, positive, proactive purpose statement. At this point, Gina is excited about writing her document. She quickly numbers the points in the order she wishes to discuss them and then dashes off her draft without a hitch.

## Using These Techniques

There you have it: six techniques to jumpstart the drafting of a document. The key to using any of these techniques for developing the points of your discussion (*area*) is to think all along about your purpose (*aim*) and your reader (*audience*). So imagine yourself in a dialogue with your readers, *speaking* to them and *listening* to their responses. Drafting, which is the topic of Chapter 3, needs to move freely to break through writer's block; therefore, you will want to have a strong plan for composing your document.

Finally, how much planning must you do before moving on to the drafting stage? Not a moment more than you need. Once you believe that you know your purpose, understand your readers, and possess enough detail to write the draft, then draft.

## Summary

We plan documents to generate ideas related to our document and to overcome writer's block. When planning, we are mindful of the 3 A's—aim, audience, area—so that we may discover our purpose, understand our audience, and collect supporting details.

Six effective planning techniques at our disposal are boilerplate, planning templates, audience surveys, idea lists, idea tags, and idea maps. All are powerful means of easing into the writing process. Choose the ones that suit your style and writing tasks.

# CHAPTER 3

# Drafting

"All that is gold does not glitter; not all those that wander are lost."

— J.R.R. Tolkien

༄

"Throw yourself off a cliff and build wings on the way down."

— Ray Bradbury

༄

"The palest ink is better than the best memory."

— Chinese proverb

This chapter describes the second step of the PDQ writing process: drafting. It is divided into two sections: the first is theoretical, and the second is practical. The theoretical section defines drafting and discusses its creative and time-management aspects. The second section offers specific suggestions for writing efficient and effective drafts.

## The Time Management of Drafting

Think for a moment about how you break the ice with someone you meet for the first time. You may smile at that person, nod, bow, or extend your hand, depending on your cultural and personal style. But this isn't all you do; you also use language. Maybe you'll say nothing more than "hello" or "how are you?" or talk about the weather. But you start using language to get the communication process going. In short, you start the speaking process by speaking.

This sounds easier than it really is. It may require overcoming *internal barriers*, such as self-consciousness, personal prejudices, language deficiencies, and subject-matter knowledge, as well as *external barriers,* such as the other person's language comprehension and attitude about you and the purpose of your meeting. Yet, we go ahead and just do it. The truth is we're so used to conversing with people that speaking comes *naturally.*

Writing is different because we're writing for readers who aren't necessarily standing in front of us. We have to assume what questions the reader might have about our topic. We might not know about the reader's attitude, interest, or knowledge about our topic. Sometimes we might not even be sure if we're writing to the correct person. Compound these problems with a general lack of confidence about our writing skills or a lack of knowledge about our topic or any other combination of anxieties that we might have about the writing situation, and we're bound to hit the wall called writer's block. Perhaps if the readers were standing beside us, they would ask the right questions to jumpstart the writing process. But they're not. So we must write alone.

Writing the first draft requires us to put aside any reservations that we might have about our readers or our reason for writing, turn to the outline we created in the planning step, and just let our thoughts fly. In other words, you start the draft by lowering your expectations of a perfect document and realize that you plan and draft your documents for just one person: yourself. So just let those fingers fly on the keyboard. To better understand drafting, consider three tips, each of which is highlighted by an aphorism in the beginning of this chapter.

1. *Feel free to ramble.* When drafting, think about the Tolkien quote, "not all those that wander are lost." Sure, you should have a plan when drafting. But even the best plans cannot anticipate everything, and even the planners occasionally stray from their plans. Thus, when drafting, if you feel yourself jumping off the track you laid down in your outline, then jump. Your outline won't disappear; you won't stray as far as you might think, especially since you have already established your aim and considered your audience in Step 1. In a sense, you are wandering with your intended readers. Meanwhile, you may discover an important new point or two about your topic as you wander. Also, feel free to air your long-winded or strangely phrased sentences. No harm done in writing an awkward sentence or two—or three or more for that matter. You'll come back to them when you edit.

2. *Let serendipity happen.* The Bradbury quote, "Throw yourself off a cliff and build wings on the way down," may sound like a madman's endorsement of suicide, but the idea works wonders for the creative mind that applies it. This quote differs from Tolkien's because here you are not wandering from a plan—you're jumping into something without a plan. This encouragement may seem to contradict what we said in Chapter 2 about the need to plan a document. But sometimes, you just want to start writing

sentences because you *hear* them—you imagine yourself in a dialogue with your readers. You want to break from your structured routine. Fine. The first thing to do is relax. Next, let your fingers fly across the keyboard. Improvise as you go along, just like Bradbury suggests by his quote. Your coherence through this first draft may surprise you. On the other hand, if you suddenly feel drained of ideas or at a loss for words, then you can always go back to Step 1—the planning step—and use any of the techniques described in Chapter 2.

3. *Commit everything to paper and nothing to memory.* The Chinese proverb "The palest ink is better than the best memory" is an apt reminder for the need to put your thoughts down on the screen or on paper. Yogi Berra could have said it: writing isn't writing until it's writing. *Pondering* about what you want to write is not writing. If the thought occurs to you—regardless of its potential tone problem or your present inability to find the right words for it—then write it down. You can fix the tone problem or find the right words later. But if you only *think* about writing it, you might forget it later. Writing sticks—better than the best memory.

Contrary to what inexperienced writers might think, these three tips make you more efficient as a writer. You will better manage the time it takes to complete a document by thinking of drafting as a purely creative phase and not one in which you labor over phrasing, sentence structure, or word choice. Save all that for the quality control phase of writing.

## The Procedure for Drafting

If you're working from a well-planned outline created in Step 1 of the writing process, you may already be close to a completed draft. The four critical requirements for this step are finding a comfortable place to write, choosing a "protected" time to write, using a preferred writing tool, and writing without pause all your ideas from start to finish—even if you know only roughly what you have to say to your reader. Let's look at these four requirements one at a time.

### Requirement 1: Finding a Comfortable Place

If any phase of the writing process requires a relaxing atmosphere, it is the creative phase—when you plan and draft your document. Chapter 2 briefly mentioned some environmental and ergonomic causes for writer's block: disagreeable temperatures, lighting, noises, and seating, among other factors. Make the area where you write as comfortable as you and your company will allow.

I can't suggest an ideal place for a writer because we all have individual tastes. For me, it's at a computer in a quiet office without background music and as few pieces of paper nearby as possible. However, few people have such luxuries at their office. They constantly contend with office mates shouting across the room, ringing phones, computer breakdowns, and other distractions. Nevertheless, I've seen people write their first draft on paper to good results. (I don't advise this practice; more about it when we get to Requirement 3.) Others write well in offices housing a hundred coworkers who continually pace past their cubicle. Others efficiently pound away at the keyboard while rock or rap music blares from speakers inches away. Still others effectively compose their drafts surrounded by mounds of paperwork. But my experience observing thousands of people write tells me that most people are like me: They prefer a tranquil environment.

This is not to say that writing in any other environment is a futile task. The fact is that if you have to draft on your laptop a report in New York's Penn Station at rush hour for a meeting with your client in a half hour, then that's what you have to do. All you can hope to do is manage your writing environment to the best of your ability. The more practice you have at writing efficiently in an ideal environment, the more likely you'll adapt to shifts from the ideal.

## Requirement 2: Choosing a Protected Time

Two time factors affecting efficient drafting come to mind: period and duration.

### Period

When during your workday are you most energetic, focused, and creative? The answers I get to this question vary as the day is long. Some folks prefer drafting at the end of the day when the phones have quieted and their office is empty; others like to get in an hour early to draft their special reports; still others eat at their desk and draft while everyone else is out to lunch.

Find the time that works best for you and call it your drafting period—the time of the day when you tune out everything else and enter your drafting zone, when all you do is write. And stick to that period as you would if you were a student attending a required first-period college writing class.

## Duration

How much time can you reasonably spend drafting a document while at maximum performance? This too is not a one-answer-fits-all situation. Some people say they lose focus after 30 minutes, and others can draft nonstop for an hour. But few people, if any, can write a steady stream of words for the entire workday. Establishing a drafting time limit may increase your writing productivity. Allowing, for instance, an entire workday to write a five-page report might not make as much sense as scheduling two or three one-hour periods for it. If you give yourself an entire workday, you may unnecessarily expand the time and forsake other important work activities that you could have completed during the same period. In addition, you are bound to face interruptions repeatedly in the course of an entire workday.

The best advice is this: the less time you spend drafting, the more productive your time will be and the better you will feel about your writing accomplishments. Just as carpenters need periodic breaks from hammering nails, and plumbers cannot crouch under sink traps for hours, so too should you acknowledge that writing taxes you physically as well as mentally. It is a demanding task that requires excellent time management skills.

## Requirement 3: Using a Preferred Writing Tool

For the most part, I draft directly at the computer on my word-processing program. Most other on-the-job writers do the same. In fact, I frequently hear corporate employees joke that they've forgotten how to write with pen or pencil because their fingers are attached to their keyboards. For sure, word-processing software has emerged as the writing tool of choice in the corporate world and even the home.

Occasionally, however, I hear corporate writers say they prefer writing off screen. A marketing executive once told me, "There's something intimidating about the computer screen. It's so perfect that I'm always focused on correcting the mistakes rather than putting down my ideas." An administrative assistant also pointed out, "I feel more creative when drafting directly on paper." The problem with this thinking, however, is that the writing still has to get onto the screen; therefore, pen-to-paper drafting adds unnecessary production time to the writing process.

Others tout the value of voice recognition software as a valuable tool for promoting fluency in writing. After all, we speak at least twice as fast as we write, so voice recognition software promises to help many people overcome writer's block. As of this writing, however, voice recognition technology has yet to provide the accuracy that writers demand. Although it is programmed to detect an astounding range of variables in inflections and pronunciations, the phrasing, punctuation, and formatting inconsistencies still cause too many writing breakdowns for most people's patience. In any event, it hasn't proved to be more efficient than typing or handwriting for most writers.

While writing directly on a computer is inarguably the quickest way to record words—even for those who do not know how to type—it would be ineffective if it causes people to stare at the screen without writing for long periods; on the other hand, if handwriting gets them started right away, then they should handwrite—but jump to the computer as fast as they can. Decide on what works better for you, and use that tool to continually pick up your composing pace.

## Requirement 4: Writing without Pause

While you will want to surface your ideas by referring to the outline you created in Step 1, some thoughts may occur to you as a disorganized mess. That's all right. The main thing is to keep the creative process flowing. Change nothing and keep moving forward. And don't let your desire to create a perfect opening stop you. This means don't waste time now looking for the right word because you won't keep your train of thought—which moves slowly enough as it is when compared to your reading, speaking, or listening speed. It's still too early in the composing process to fuss over perfection. If you can't think of a good opener, start with the middle—the details—and return to the opener later.

Sometimes you may discover that your whole purpose changes as you move along through the first draft. This too is fine because good drafting often introduces you to ideas that you hadn't previously confronted. Just stay focused on the writing task. Don't even spend time reading what you've written. Some writers turn off the automatic spell-check feature in their word processor to prevent the red squiggly underlining from appearing and distracting them. Others just type and turn off the monitor. Whatever it takes. By the time you have written your draft, you'll see that some of your content is usable and some of it is not. But far worse than this minor problem is having little or nothing on the screen or page to revise, edit, and proofread.

## Two Examples

Now that we've covered the requirements of the draft, let's see two examples of what a workable—though far from perfect—first draft might look like. Each comes from a planning situation in Chapter 2, and each has different problems typical of a first draft. (More about improving these drafts in Chapter 4.)

### FIGURE 3-1
### FIRST OF FIVE DRAFTS OF
### AN INTERNAL PROPOSAL E-MAIL

*(See Figure 2-5, Sample Planning Template, for an outline of this draft.)*

**Date:** Friday, May 6, 2005, 3:07 p.m. EDT

**To:** Myra Schreiber, Manager

**From:** Bobby Aldomori

**Re:** Recommendation for Weekly IT Team Meeting

**CC:** Jason Jeffers, Manager, Information Technology Team

I would like to propose a weekly meeting with our group and the Information Technology Team. As you know, our server has crashed three times in the past month, preventing us from making the necessary changes to our website in a timely manner. This has created two problems: First, two of our clients, Eastern Focus and North Star Industries, have complained about receiving outdated information. Second, our three web designers were idle for between two and three hours during each of these incidents.

I believe that IT service has worsened since the recent acquisition of the Frost Group's IT team. We need to point out to IT that since the merger, the two IT groups have not provided consistently integrated, prompt, and effective troubleshooting services. By holding a weekly status meeting with IT, we can create and regularly review a checklist covering all pending troubleshooting efforts and planned server updates. This meeting should result in our providing more reliable and prompt responses to our clients' requests for information, experiencing less downtime, and enjoying a better working relationship with IT. As for IT, they will benefit by growing their reputation for client service and eventually freeing up a lot of their troubleshooting time through good planning and preventive maintenance.

If you think this is a good idea, I'll begin the process by creating an IT checklist that lists our common IT problems and checkpoints. In addition, I'll set up a meeting with Jason Jeffers to plan the first weekly meeting. Thanks for your consideration.

The first draft, Figure 3-1, is from Figure 2-5, the Sample Planning Template. The draft presents a good amount of information for the reader; however, it poses at least four revising challenges for the writer:

1. The purpose statement is emotionally soft (*I would like to propose a weekly meeting…*).
2. The paragraphing is ineffective. Paragraphs 2 and 3 contain more than one focused idea.
3. The lack of business-style formatting (headings and bullets) makes accessing the ideas difficult.
4. The negative focus on the IT Team's weak performance in Paragraph 2 would possibly cause the IT manager to become defensive and resistant to the writer's suggestions.

Nevertheless, the writer has written a first draft ready for quality controlling.

The next draft, Figure 3-2, is from Figure 2-6, the Sample Audience Survey. It has several strengths, including an ambitious viewpoint and an expression of willingness to help the process along. However, it has at least eight weaknesses:

1. It lacks a purpose statement in the opening.
2. It lacks clearly stated next steps in the closing.
3. The ideas are poorly organized because the first three paragraphs contain more than one idea.
4. A failure to format the memo with headings and bullets makes the document difficult to access.
5. Some sentences in the second and third paragraphs lack solid transitions.
6. The writer uses wordy expressions, such as "could not be occurring at a more difficult time," "your interesting and indisputable point," and "please call me if you have any questions."
7. Potential tone problems might arise—though unintended by the writer. She suggests that her unit is being pressured by Human Resources to do more than it can, that the manager did not adequately plan for the summer project by allowing four associates to vacation at a peak production period, and that she is prepared to plan before the manager is.
8. The writer uses absolutes ("surpasses all other matters" in the second paragraph and "completely solve" in the last paragraph), which shows an intellectual laziness on her part.

## FIGURE 3-2
## FIRST OF FIVE DRAFTS OF
## AN INTERNAL PROPOSAL MEMORANDUM

*(See Figure 2-6, Sample Audience Survey, for an outline of this draft.)*

MEMORANDUM

**To:**       Monica Ruiz
**From:**     Cori Parlin
**Date:**     February 8, 2005
**Subject:**  Request for a Summer Intern

Since four of our five associates will vacation at different times in July and August, we can expect to have inadequate coverage during the summer months. This could not be occurring at a more difficult time, as Human Resources has requested that our unit assume increased responsibilities by providing training material for its new-hire orientation program, when the Company will process approximately 150 recently graduated new employees.

Although we have not yet planned how to meet this increased production require-ment, we spoke at our last weekly meeting about how we may be inadequately staffed to achieve the performance level expected of our group. Your interesting and indisputable point during that meeting—that we should impress our new hires with an efficient orientation process—was an excellent one that I believe surpasses all other matters. This is why hiring an intern may be a solution to our problem. It may be possible to look into recruiting one from either New York College or City Acad-emy. This may also offer the additional benefit of opening relations with the placement offices of these two colleges.

During our orientation season, from May 31 through August 19, an intern would be able to help in a variety of functions, including the typing of training manuals, photocopying of materials, researching of training resources on the Internet, distributing of materials, creating of a new associate database, and covering on our main phone line. Jillian Weinstein has mentioned to me that she would be happy to supervise the intern's work. In checking with Human Resources, I learned that the Company's standard intern rate is $15 per hour, which seems to be well within our budget.

I could begin the hiring process by April 18, and we will completely solve this production problem, provided the idea is accepted by March 28. Please call me if you have any questions.

Nevertheless, the writer's rough draft is an excellent one to begin quality controlling in Step 3 of the PDQ writing process. We'll see how she tackles this draft in Chapter 4.

## Two Final Thoughts

To ensure that your drafts fly from your brain through your fingers to the screen or page, remember these two final thoughts: first, read to write, and second, write a lot.

### Read to Write

Good writing emerges from good reading. Read as much as you can from literature about your field, from the commonly accepted model documents in your company, and from sources outside your field—especially if your company serves a diverse client base.

What we read instructs us about the standards to strive toward and inspires us to sit down and write. So the next time you feel writer's block over a critical client proposal, step back from the computer and pick up the last proposal that impressed you; the next time you feel stressed over meeting minutes that you must get out by the afternoon, review those meeting minutes you wrote last month. Or just read any author who moves you to write, in the same way that a casual golfer becomes inspired by a Tiger Woods drive onto the green, or a weekend tennis player gets the itch to play after watching a Serena Williams serve. Just as the golfer and tennis player aren't seeking to rise to the level of Woods or Williams, the on-the-job writer doesn't have to seek perfection when writing the first draft.

### Write a Lot

Keeping a hard-copy notebook or an electronic journal of your daily activities or observations, or even a record of your planning and drafting, promotes writing fluency, which is the goal of the first two steps of the PDQ writing process. Writing every day in a journal is no different from an athlete practicing or an entertainer rehearsing; it helps you stay fresh and capable of writing on demand. When writing in a journal, remember that quality is not as important as quantity. No one but you—and often not even you!—needs to read your journal. It's there as your mental gymnasium. The more the fingers move, the more they're used to moving and connecting your brain to the screen or page.

# Summary

Drafting is Step 2 of the writing process. When drafting, feel free to ramble, don't become too dependent on your plan, and write down as much as your brain can surface. The goal of drafting is to write efficiently. To ensure that your drafts achieve efficiency, find a comfortable place to write, choose a relaxed time of day and a suitable duration, write with whatever tool is most convenient to you—preferably the computer—and write without pause or correcting your mistakes. Reading a lot and practicing your writing will also strengthen your writing fluency.

# CHAPTER 4

# Revising

"Reading makes a full man, conference a ready man, and writing an exact man."

– Francis Bacon

"I have only made this letter longer because I have not had the time to make it shorter."

– Blaise Pascal

"Ideas won't keep; something must be done about them."

– Alfred North Whitehead

This chapter describes the third step of the PDQ writing process: quality controlling. It then focuses on revising—the quality controlling of the writer's ideas—by showing how to use the 4S Plan: statement, support, structure, and style.

## The Need for Quality Controlling Your Documents

Often, after writers in my corporate courses have completed a rough draft, I ask, "How do you know that you're finished?" The answers are usually on target: "I know I'm finished when I've written down everything that was in the outline I created during the planning stage." "I'm finished because my brain is spent and I can't think of anything else to write about." "I'm done because I'm itching to fix it up now." All fine answers.

The certainty in the room diminishes when I then ask, "So what's the first thing to do when you quality control?" Answers range from, "I scream 'Help!'" to "I don't know, so that's why I'm here."

This chapter and the next two describe in sequential detail a methodical approach to quality controlling the document. The techniques described will contribute to your writing efficiency. As noted in previous chapters, we plan and draft only for ourselves, but we quality control to protect our REP: Thus, we *revise* the ideas we want to communicate, *edit* the expression of those ideas, and *proofread* a hard copy for overlooked errors, in that order. And we begin revising with our purpose and audience in mind. In fact, we cannot think of what we want to say without also thinking of whom we're saying it to. Let Figure 4-1 remind you that your purpose and audience are inseparable, and that imbedded in your purpose is your audience and vice versa.

**FIGURE 4-1**
**KEYS TO QUALITY CONTROLLING**
**ON-THE-JOB DOCUMENTS**

*Purpose*

*Audience*

Revising represents a critical moment in the writing process—some writing experts say it is the most critical moment—because at this point you CARE for your reader. In other words, revising calls for you to change, add, reorganize/reformat, or eliminate the ideas of the document all at the service of your readers. Figure 4-2 illustrates the functions of revision.

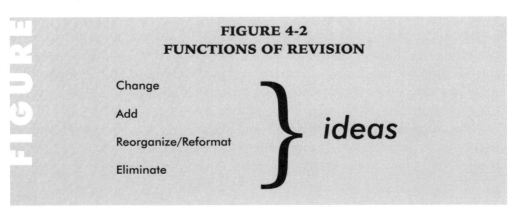

**FIGURE 4-2**
**FUNCTIONS OF REVISION**

Change

Add

Reorganize/Reformat

Eliminate

} *ideas*

# The 4S Plan

When revising, you will want to check your document by using the 4S Plan (Figure 4-3): the *statement, support, structure,* and *style.* Broadly speaking, these four domains cover the following qualities:

· Statement: purposefulness
· Support: completeness
· Structure: organization and format
· Style: content-context balance

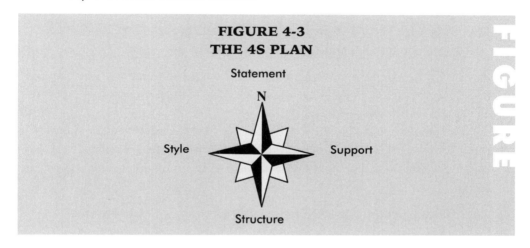

**FIGURE 4-3**
**THE 4S PLAN**

Statement

Style

Support

Structure

Let's move through the 4S Plan by working on the two sample documents from Chapters 2 and 3. As noted in Chapter 3, these two drafts are workable but far from perfect. By viewing them through the revision phase of the quality-control step, you will see many of the decisions successful writers must make to ensure that they are delivering their message.

## Statement

On-the-job documents need two elements to be clear in purpose:

1. a purpose statement, which speaks for the entire document
2. next steps, which transition the reader from the document to the desired results

The purpose statement should appear in a single sentence. I often call it the "mother sentence" because it is the highest-level sentence in the document, and it speaks for every other sentence in the document. Too often, writers weaken the power of their documents by making one or both of the following mistakes:

1. They omit the purpose statement in the document because they believe that their subject line does the job by previewing the purpose. For example, they may write in the subject line, "Re: Recommendation for Weekly IT Team Meeting" but fail to state in the document "I recommend a weekly IT meeting."
2. They only imply the purpose, thinking that works just as well as an explicit one. For example, they may write, "A weekly meeting with the IT Team would benefit our group as well as IT" but not actually state their recommendation.

Although the purpose statement is only a single sentence, writers should not underestimate its power in guiding them toward creating a complete, clear, and consistent message.

The next steps are equally important because rather than close the document with a this-is-how-I-feel statement, they move the idea along. Inexperienced writers make at least one of three common mistakes with their next steps:

1. *They omit them altogether*, preferring just to summarize what they had just said. For example, they might write, "Therefore, a weekly meeting with the IT Team would benefit our organization."
2. *They understate them*, writing a vague statement like "Please call me if you have questions about this recommendation," which requires nothing of the reader.
3. *They misplace them.* They may write, "I will forward to you a possible agenda for the first weekly meeting," which seems effective; however, they may bury it in the middle of the document instead of placing it where it belongs—at the end.

Next steps are critical to the document because they serve as the call to action. Writers often express anxiety about writing next steps because they feel that they must inappropriately demand something of their readers, who may be a level or more above them. But they should think of next steps not as something that their readers should do; maybe the writer can take the next steps himself. For instance, instead of ending with, "I look forward to

**FIGURE 4-4**
**PROCEDURE FOR CHECKING THE STATEMENT**

| Step | Ask | If Yes | If No |
|------|-----|--------|-------|
| 1 | Do I have a purpose statement? | Highlight it and go to Step 2. | Create a purpose statement. |
| 2 | Does the purpose statement speak for the entire document? | Go to Step 3. | Revise it so that it does. |
| 3 | Is the purpose statement at the top of the document? | Go to Step 4. | Place it at the top. |
| 4 | Does the purpose statement belong at the top of the document? | Go to Step 5. | Move it down one sentence at a time until it belongs. |
| 5 | Do I have next steps? | Go to Step 6. | Create next steps. |
| 6 | Are the next steps consistent with my purpose statement? | Go to Step 7. | Revise them so that they are consistent with the purpose. |
| 7 | Are the next steps at the end of the document? | You have checked the statement. | Place them at the end of the document. |

your response to my recommendation," why not close with, "I'll call you on Tuesday to discuss this recommendation"?

Figure 4-4 serves as a flow chart for identifying and refining the purpose statement and next steps of the document. Let's use it to revise the statement of the two sample documents from Chapter 3. I noted in Chapter 3 that Bobby Aldomori's draft (Figure 4-5) had an emotionally soft purpose statement, and that Cori Parlin's draft (Figure 4-6) had no purpose statement at all.

## FIGURE 4-5
## REVISING THE FIRST DRAFT FOR THE STATEMENT

**Date:** Friday, May 6, 2005, 3:07 p.m. EDT
**To:** Myra Schreiber, Manager
**From:** Bobby Aldomori
**Re:** Recommendation for Weekly IT Team Meeting
**CC:** Jason Jeffers, Manager, Information Technology Team

Step 1: Highlight the purpose statement

I would like to propose a weekly meeting with our group and the Information Technology Team. As you know, our server has crashed three times in the past month, preventing us from making the necessary changes to our website in a timely manner. This has created two problems: First, two of our clients, Eastern Focus and North Star Industries, have complained about receiving outdated information. Second, our three web designers were idle for between two and three hours during each of these incidents.

I believe that IT service has worsened since the recent acquisition of the Frost Group's IT team. We need to point out to IT that since the merger, the two IT groups have not provided consistently integrated, prompt, and effective troubleshooting services. By holding a weekly status meeting with IT, we can create and regularly review a checklist covering all pending troubleshooting efforts and planned server updates. This meeting should result in our providing more reliable and prompt responses to our clients' requests for information, experiencing less downtime, and enjoying a better working relationship with IT. As for IT, they will benefit by growing their reputation for client service and ev    Step 5: Highlight the next steps.    eir trouble-shooting time through good planning and

If you think this is a good idea, I'll begin the process by creating an IT checklist that lists our common IT problems and checkpoints. In addition, I'll set up a meeting with Jason Jeffers to plan the first weekly meeting. Thanks for your consideration.

# FIGURE 4-6
## REVISING THE FIRST DRAFT FOR THE STATEMENT

MEMORANDUM

**To:** Monica Ruiz
**From:** Cori Parlin
**Date:** Februrary 28, 2005
**Subject:** Request for a Summer Intern

> Step 1: Create and highlight the purpose statement.

I ask that you consider hiring a summer intern to help our group efficiently manage the new-hire orientation program. Since four of our five associates will vacation at different times in July and August, we can expect to have inadequate coverage during the summer months. This could not be occurring at a more difficult time, as Human Resources has requested that our unit assume increased responsibilities by providing training material for its new-hire orientation program, when the Company will process approximately 150 recently graduated new employees.

Although we have not yet planned how to meet this increased production requirement, we spoke at our last weekly meeting about how we may be inadequately staffed to achieve the performance level expected of our group. Your interesting and indisputable point during that meeting—that we should impress our new hires with an efficient orientation process—was an excellent one that I believe surpasses all other matters. This is why hiring an intern may be a solution to our problem. It may be possible to look into recruiting one from either New York College or City Academy. This may also offer the additional benefit of opening relations with the placement offices of these two colleges.

During our orientation season, from May 31 through August 19, an intern would be able to help in a variety of functions, including the typing of training manuals, photocopying of materials, researching of training resources on the Internet, distributing of materials, creating of a new associate database, and covering on our main phone line. Jillian Weinstein has mentioned to me that she would be happy to supervise the intern's work. In checking with Human Resources, I learned that the Company's standard intern rate is $15 per hour, which see budget.

> Step 5: Highlight the next steps.

I could begin the hiring process by April 18, and we will completely solve this production problem, provided the idea is accepted by March 28. Please call me if you have any questions.

## Step 1

Step 1 is easy enough for Bobby. He highlights his purpose statement in Figure 4-5. Cori, on the other hand, has no purpose statement, so she creates one in Figure 4-6.

## Step 2

Step 2 calls for the writer to measure every word of the purpose statement for accuracy. The writer should ensure that:

1. the sentence broadly previews the content to follow
2. every other sentence in the document points to this one

Bobby adds context language to motivate the reader and eliminates three unnecessary words to tighten it:

> *In an effort to improve our client service,* I ~~would like to~~ propose a weekly meeting with our group and the Information Technology Team.

Cori believes that her manager may forward the memo to the Vice-president and the Director of Human Resources, who both maintain a more formal relationship with Cori's unit, so she decides to make her purpose statement less personal:

> To manage the new-hire orientation program efficiently, the Publications Unit requests the full-time services of a summer intern.

## Step 3

Both Bobby and Cori answer "yes" to the Step 3 question, "Is the purpose statement at the top of the document?"

## Step 4

However useful the purpose statement is at the top of the document (it's easy for the reader to reference), it may not always be appropriate at the top. The placement of the purpose depends upon the writer's relationship with the readers and their connection to the purpose. Work-related documents are much like dialogues. When we expect to have a direct dialogue with someone, we can get to the point immediately. Most business documents are like direct dialogues; therefore, their purpose statement appears at the top. Examples of direct messages are:

- instructions
- product descriptions
- meeting minutes
- most routine requests
- most responses to routine requests
- root-cause analyses
- trip reports
- employee evaluations and self-evaluations
- invitations
- most reminders
- requests for proposals
- solicited proposals
- some unsolicited proposals

However, we may delay the point of the discussion in two situations:

1. When delivering bad news, such as a rejection letter.
2. When delivering a message that our audience might reject, such as a proposal for purchasing an expensive product during a budget crisis.

In such cases, we would not want to bury our purpose at the bottom of the message, but we may delay it by beginning with an expression of sympathy before the bad news, or the reason before the request. Again, we base this decision entirely on our relationship with the reader and our connection to the purpose. Consider, for instance, the following two examples (the purpose statements are highlighted):

EXAMPLE 1: Gloria, a manager, directs Ralph, a subordinate, by e-mail. She begins her message with the purpose statement because she feels comfortable directing him in a straightforward manner.

---

Ralph,

Please submit the quarterly sales report by next Thursday. We need it two weeks earlier than usual because the new Vice-president, Darcy Coleman, has requested it for her stockholder presentation on June 18.

Thank you.

Gloria

---

EXAMPLE 2: Ralph sees a problem with this request because he will need his manager's help, but he wants to assure her that his first interest is in fulfilling it. Therefore, he begins his e-mail with a positive opening and follows with his reason before his request for help.

---

Gloria,

Thank you for the advance notice. I already have begun compiling the sales projections data for the report and expect to have them completed on time. However, the second quarter sales figures are due from the Sales Division on June 27. To make the quarterly report as comprehensive as possible, I see two possible options:

1. Submit precise sales numbers for April and May only and estimate June based on a year-by-year comparison.

2. Request from the Sales Division an "official estimate" based on its tentative figures.

Regardless of the option you choose, I will need your assistance in completing the report for the following reasons:

If you choose Option 1, my June comparison to last year may be unreliable because of the projected sales increase resulting from the Candy2.0 launch. I'd need your guidance on projecting the percentage increase.

If you choose Option 2, Sales has in the past not responded to these requests promptly, so I would suggest that the request come from Darcy's office. If you'd like, I could draft a request for her within an hour of your response and forward it to you for any revision.

Please let me know which option you prefer, or if other options exist, and how I should proceed.

Thanks,

Ralph

---

Let's return to Bobby's e-mail in Figure 4-5 and Cori's memo in Figure 4-6. In placing his purpose, Bobby imagines himself walking into an office and finding his primary reader (his manager Myra) and his secondary readers (IT Manager Jason and members of Bobby's group). He asks himself, "Would I enter the office saying, 'In an effort to improve our client service, I propose a weekly meeting with our group and the Information Technology Team'?" He decides that his relationship to the purpose and with all these people would warrant a direct approach; therefore, he answers, "yes" to the question, "Does the purpose statement belong at the top of the document?"

The placement of Cori's purpose yields a different response. She also imagines herself walking into an office and finding her primary reader (her manager Monica) and her secondary readers (Vice-president Christine, Director of Human Resources Carlos, and teammate Jillian). She asks herself, "Would I enter the office saying, 'To manage the new-hire orientation program efficiently, the Publications Unit requests the full-time services of a summer intern'?" She decides that such an approach would appear too aggressive to the vice-president and the director, who hardly know her; therefore, she opts for an indirect approach. She moves her purpose statement down a sentence at a time until she feels comfortable with its placement. Now her opening looks like this:

> ~~Since four of our five associates will vacation at different times in July and August, we can expect to have inadequate coverage during the summer months. This could not be occurring at a more difficult time, as~~ Human Resources has requested that our unit assume increased responsibilities by providing training material for its new-hire orientation program, when the Company will process approximately 150 recently graduated new employees. To manage the ~~new-hire orientation~~ program efficiently, the Publications Unit requests the full-time services of a summer intern.

Notice that by moving the purpose statement, Cori also made the following three changes:

1. Eliminated the tone problem that might arise without at least a transition to the fact that four of five associates will take summer vacations. (Cori is still deciding whether to include this information later in the document. This is an issue she will address when checking the second S—*support.*)
2. Eliminated the wordy, negative, and inaccurate expression "This could not be occurring at a more difficult time."

3. Eliminated from it the now-redundant phrase "new-hire orientation."

### Step 5

Bobby answers *yes* to the question, "Do I have next steps?" and he highlights them. (See Figure 4-5.) Cori also answers *yes* to the question, "Do I have next steps?" and she highlights them. (See Figure 4-6.)

### Step 6

Answering the question, "Are the next steps consistent with my purpose statement?" requires that writers compare the purpose and next steps to determine whether they connect logically—again, based on the readers' needs. Some documents state their purpose clearly in the beginning of the document but fail to follow through with clear next steps in the ending; others open weakly but deliver solid next steps. The way to fix either problem is to compare the purpose and next steps. Below are examples of each situation.

STRONG PURPOSE, WEAK NEXT STEPS:

*Purpose:* I am requesting your support in installing our group's new word processing software package.
*Next steps:* Call me if you have any question.

While the opening sets up a clear expectation from the writer, the next steps do not provide a call to action for the reader.

WEAK PURPOSE, STRONG NEXT STEPS:

*Purpose:* I have been trying to install our group's new word processing software package.
*Next steps:* I will call you tomorrow at 10:00 a.m. to set up an installation schedule convenient to you.

While the closing provides the clear call to action, the reader might not expect it because the writer never explicitly stated that he needs the reader's help. The best approach would be for the writer in the first example to use the purpose statement to strengthen his next steps, and for the writer in the second example to use his next steps to clarify his purpose statement.

Bobby looks at his revised purpose statement and his next steps:

| Purpose: | In an effort to improve our client service and create a seamless working relationship with the Information Technology Team, I propose a weekly meeting with our group and IT. |
|---|---|
| Next steps: | If you think this is a good idea, I'll begin the process by creating an IT checklist that lists our common IT problems and checkpoints. In addition, I'll set up a meeting with Jason Jeffers to plan the first weekly meeting. |

He sees that the next steps move the purpose along just the way he would like, so he leaves them unchanged.

Cori looks at her revised purpose statement and her next steps:

| Purpose: | To manage the program efficiently, the Publications Unit requests the full-time services of a summer intern. |
|---|---|
| Next steps: | I could begin the hiring process by April 18, and we will completely solve this production problem, provided the idea is accepted by March 28. Please call me if you have any questions. |

She identifies four problems with these next steps:

1. They are not specific enough in moving along the hiring process.
2. Her claim of "completely" solving the production problem is overstated.
3. The March 28 deadline seems too pushy for the impersonal, formal style she wants to convey.
4. Her last sentence is useless.

Cori revises her next steps to read:

> If the Publications Unit receives management approval to hire the summer intern by March 28, Jillian can begin interviewing applicants from the Human Resources candidate bank by April 18 and select three final candidates for management approval by April 25. Publications appreciates the opportunity to present this proposal and is prepared to assist in the decision making process, if needed.

### Step 7

Both Bobby and Cori answer yes to the question, "Are the next steps at the end of the document?" Now they are ready to move on to the second S—*support*. Figures 4-7 and 4-8 show their documents revised for the statement.

For practice, see Exercise 4-1 on page 129.

## FIGURE 4-7
## THE STATEMENT—SECOND OF FIVE DRAFTS

**Date:** Friday, May 6, 2005, 3:07 p.m. EDT

**To:** Myra Schreiber, Manager

**From:** Bobby Aldomori

**Re:** Recommendation for Weekly IT Team Meeting

**CC:** Jason Jeffers, Manager, Information Technology Team

In an effort to improve our client service and create a seamless working relationship with the Information Technology Team, I propose a weekly meeting with our group and IT. As you know, our server has crashed three times in the past month, preventing us from making the necessary changes to our website in a timely manner. This has created two problems: First, two of our clients, Eastern Focus and North Star Industries, have complained about receiving outdated information. Second, our three web designers were idle for between two and three hours during each of these incidents.

I believe that IT service has worsened since the recent acquisition of the Frost Group's IT team. We need to point out to IT that since the merger, the two IT groups have not provided consistently integrated, prompt, and effective troubleshooting services. By holding a weekly status meeting with IT, we can create and regularly review a checklist covering all pending troubleshooting efforts and planned server updates. This meeting should result in our providing more reliable and prompt responses to our clients' requests for information, experiencing less downtime, and enjoying a better working relationship with IT. As for IT, they will benefit by growing their reputation for client service and eventually freeing up a lot of their troubleshooting time through good planning and preventive maintenance.

If you think this is a good idea, I'll begin the process by creating an IT checklist that lists our common IT problems and checkpoints. In addition, I'll set up a meeting with Jason Jeffers to plan the first weekly meeting. Thanks for your consideration.

# FIGURE 4-8
## THE STATEMENT—SECOND OF FIVE DRAFTS

MEMORANDUM

**To:** Monica Ruiz
**From:** Cori Parlin
**Date:** February 8, 2005
**Subject:** Request for a Summer Intern

Human Resources has requested that our unit assume increased responsibilities by providing training material for its new-hire orientation program, when the Company will process approximately 150 recently graduated new employees. To manage the program efficiently, the Publications Unit requests the full-time services of a summer intern.

Although we have not yet planned how to meet this increased production require-ment, we spoke at our last weekly meeting about how we may be inadequately staffed to achieve the performance level expected of our group. Your interesting and indisput-able point during that meeting—that we should impress our new hires with an efficient orientation process—was an excellent one that I believe surpasses all other matters. This is why hiring an intern may be a solution to our problem. It may be possible to look into recruiting one from either New York College or City Academy. This may also offer the additional benefit of opening relations with the placement offices of these two colleges.

During our orientation season, from May 31 through August 19, an intern would be able to help in a variety of functions, including the typing of training manuals, photocopying of materials, researching of training resources on the Internet, distributing of materials, creating of a new associate database, and covering on our main phone line. Jillian Weinstein has mentioned to me that she would be happy to supervise the intern's work. In checking with Human Resources, I learned that the Company's standard intern rate is $15 per hour, which seems to be well within our budget.

If the Publications Unit receives management approval to hire the summer intern by March 28, Jillian can begin interviewing applicants from the Human Resources candidate bank by April 18 and select three final candidates for management approval by April 25. Publications appreciates the opportunity to present this proposal and is prepared to assist in the decision making process, if needed.

## Support

The statement focuses the readers on the writer's purpose; the support addresses any concern the readers might have about the writer's purpose. As noted in Chapter 1, the wider the audience, the more concerns the writer must address. The best way to determine those concerns is to know your audience and their relationship to your purpose.

Some business writers like to refer to the supporting details as the *who, what, when, where, why,* and *how* of the document—also known as the *5W+H.* The 5W+H is a good start, but it's not enough. Thinking of these six elements as a set might cause a writer to assume that they are of equal value. However, their value varies depending on the writer's purpose and the audience's concerns. The *how* may be unnecessary in some documents; in others, the *who* may be a single word or phrase, while the *why* may be three pages long; still others may be all about *what.*

One helpful way to determine the supporting details is to imagine yourself in a dialogue with the readers as they sit across a table from you. What would they ask or say in response to your comments? In other words, work your document in reverse, as if your sentences were in reaction to what your readers were saying. Let's use Bobby's and Cori's documents to see how this method would unfold.

First, Bobby imagines himself in a conference room with his manager Myra, the Information Technology Manager Jason, and Helen and Kurt, two members of his group. Referring to Figures 4-7 and 4-9, notice that the italicized words in Bobby's dialogue actually appear in his original draft, the boldfaced words are added to it, the crossed out words are eliminated, and the normal font is just conversation that wouldn't appear in a document.

---

### FIGURE 4-9
### CHECKING FOR THE SUPPORT

Bobby:   Good morning, folks.

All:   Good morning.

Bobby:   As I mentioned to you in my voice mail, I'd like to discuss a way *to improve client service and create a seamless working relationship with the Information Technology Team.* That's why we invited Jason to this meeting. Welcome, Jason.

## FIGURE 4-9 CONT.
## CHECKING FOR THE SUPPORT

Jason: Thanks for having me.

Myra: What have you got for us, Bobby?

Bobby: *I propose a weekly meeting with our group and IT.*

Kurt: (Lightheartedly:) Ugh. Just what we need. Another meeting.

Jason: What would be its purpose?

Bobby: *As you know, our server has crashed three times in the past month.*

Jason: I realize that. **It put us back a whole week in our new anti-virus software installation package.**

Bobby: And it *prevented us from making the necessary changes to our website in a timely manner.*

Jason: With all the hardware vendor problems I have now, the last thing I need is another regularly scheduled meeting.

Bobby: I understand that. Some meetings accomplish nothing and distract us from our work. But these crashes *have created two problems* for our team: *First, two of our clients, Eastern Focus and North Star Industries, have complained about receiving outdated information. And second, our three web designers were idle for between two and three hours during each of these incidents.*

Myra: This translates to over a thousand dollars in productivity per outage, Jason. And that doesn't include dealing with disappointed customers.

Jason: But I don't see how our meeting once a week will solve anything. We're working around the clock as it is. My people are averaging sixty to seventy hours a week and half of them are on call twenty-four seven. And don't forget all the training time we're into because of the merger with Frost Group.

Bobby: ~~I believe that IT service has worsened since the recent ac-quisition of the Frost Group's IT team. We need to point out to IT that since the merger, the two IT groups have not provided consistently integrated, prompt, and effective troubleshooting services.~~ I realize that, Jason, just as I'm

**FIGURE 4-9** CONT.
**CHECKING FOR THE SUPPORT**

|         |                                                                                                                                                                                                                                         |
|---------|-----------------------------------------------------------------------------------------------------------------------------------------------------------------------------------------------------------------------------------------|
|         | sure that **you're committed to providing us with consistently integrated, prompt, and effective troubleshooting services.**                                                                                                             |
| Jason:  | Of course I am. What would the meeting cover?                                                                                                                                                                                           |
| Bobby:  | *By holding a weekly status meeting with IT, we can create and regularly review a checklist covering all pending troubleshooting efforts and planned server updates.*                                                                   |
| Jason:  | I'm really tight for time.                                                                                                                                                                                                               |
| Kurt:   | Aren't we all!                                                                                                                                                                                                                           |
| Helen:  | If we had these meetings, how long would they run?                                                                                                                                                                                     |
| Bobby:  | **Meetings should run no longer than thirty minutes.**                                                                                                                                                                                  |
| Jason:  | OK. But time is an issue. The only available time I have is at the crack of dawn.                                                                                                                                                        |
| Bobby:  | **We could begin at eight a.m. before everyone's normal business rush hours.**                                                                                                                                                           |
| Kurt:   | Would you want all of us to attend?                                                                                                                                                                                                      |
| Bobby:  | **Only the manager and an associate representing each group on a rotating basis should attend. They should be sufficient to keep the teams abreast of the latest IT developments affecting their group.**                                |
| Myra:   | I think that *this meeting should result in our providing more reliable and prompt responses to our clients' requests for information* and *experiencing less downtime.* Another benefit is that we would *enjoy a better working relationship with* you and your group, Jason. **We never really get to share common concerns, so this meeting would be an ideal way for us to connect on a professional level.** |
| Bobby:  | Also, *IT associates would benefit by growing their reputation for client service and eventually freeing up a lot of their troubleshooting time through good planning and preventive maintenance.*                                      |
| Jason:  | Fine.                                                                                                                                                                                                                                    |
| Myra:   | What's the next step here, Bobby?                                                                                                                                                                                                        |
| Bobby:  | ~~If you think this is a good idea,~~ *I'll begin the process by creating an IT checklist that lists our common IT problems and checkpoints.*                                                                                             |

**FIGURE 4-9** CONT.
**CHECKING FOR THE SUPPORT**

Myra: Good. But can we set a time for the first meeting now?

Jason: You bet.

Bobby ~~In addition, I'll set up a meeting with Jason Jeffers to plan the first weekly meeting.~~

Jason: Next Thursday at eight, then?

Bobby: Great. *Thanks for ~~your consideration~~ taking the time* to help us, Jason.

Let's examine the revisions that Bobby makes:

1. He changes the negative criticism of the IT Team, which may upset Jason, to a positive goal that is more likely to win Jason's agreement.
2. He adds information that he thinks his readers need to know:
   - the problem that the server crashes have caused the IT Team
   - the duration of the meeting
   - the usual time of the meeting
   - who will attend the meeting
   - an additional mutual benefit of the meeting

Bobby's draft revised for *support* appears in Figure 4-10.

**FIGURE 4-10**
**THE SUPPORT—THIRD OF FIVE DRAFTS**

**Date:** Tuesday, May 6, 2005, 3:07 p.m. EDT
**To:** Myra Schreiber, Manager
**From:** Bobby Aldomori
**Re:** Recommendation for Weekly IT Team Meeting
**CC:** Jason Jeffers, Manager, Information Technology Team

In an effort to improve our client service and create a seamless working relationship with the Information Technology Team, I propose a weekly meeting with our group and IT. As you know, our server has crashed three times in the past month, preventing us from making the necessary changes to our website in a timely manner. This has created two problems: First, two of our clients, Eastern Focus and North Star Industries, have complained about receiving outdated information. Second, our three web designers were idle for between two and three hours during each of these

**FIGURE 4-10 cont.**
**THE SUPPORT—THIRD OF FIVE DRAFTS**

incidents. In addition, the IT Team has had to delay by a week the installation of its new anti-virus software installation package.

I believe that IT is committed to providing us with consistently integrated, prompt, and effective troubleshooting services. By holding a weekly status meeting with IT, we can create and regularly review a checklist covering all pending troubleshooting efforts and planned server updates. Meetings should not run more than a half hour, and we can hold them at 8:00 a.m. before everyone's normal business rush hours, or at another mutually convenient time. Only the manager and an associate representing each group on a rotating basis would need to attend. They should be sufficient to keep the teams abreast of the latest IT developments affecting their group. This meeting should result in our providing more reliable and prompt responses to our clients' requests for information and experiencing less downtime. In addition, our group and IT would enjoy a better working relationship by sharing common concerns and meeting regularly on a professional level. IT associates would also benefit by growing their reputation for client service and eventually freeing up a lot of their troubleshooting time through good planning and preventive maintenance.

To begin this process, I would create an IT checklist that lists our common IT problems and checkpoints. In addition, I would set up a meeting with Jason Jeffers to plan the first weekly meeting. Thank you for your consideration.

Now let's look at Cori's memo. Cori imagines herself in an office talking with Monica, her manager; Christine, the Vice-president, who is also Monica's manager; Carlos, Director of Human Resources; and Jillian, Cori's teammate. As you follow along in Figure 4-11, remember that the italicized words actually appear in Cori's original draft, the boldfaced words are added to it, the crossed out words are eliminated, and the normal font is just conversation that wouldn't appear in the message.

For practice, see Exercise 4-2 on page 131.

Here's a quick review of Cori's changes:

1. She finally decides not to raise the issue of staff vacations, preferring to use the increased workload as her major selling point.
2. She eliminates any suggestions that Monica is unprepared to deal with this issue.
3. She researches in detail the workload required as a result of the new-hire orientation program.

4. She concedes that one of the four projects can be outsourced or modified. Cori will now write this concession into the document as a sign that her group has already made a sincere effort to cut operating expenses.

5. She eliminates some of the pompous sounding "Your interesting and indisputable point during that meeting," the trite sounding "we should impress our new hires with an efficient orientation process," and the unconditional sounding "an excellent (idea) that I believe surpasses all other matters."

6. She reorganizes the idea about hiring from a college.

**FIGURE 4-11**
**CHECKING FOR THE SUPPORT**

Monica: Thanks for coming to this meeting.

All: Good to be here ... Thanks for having me ... etc.

Monica: As you know, I've asked you to stop by this morning because Cori has identified a production problem in the Publications Unit and believes that she has a solution for it. Cori?

Cori: Thanks, Monica. As you know, Carlos ~~has requested that our unit assume increased responsibilities by~~ *provide training materials for its new-hire orientation program, when the Company will process approximately 150 recently graduated new employees.*

Carlos: Yes. It's our biggest and most important orientation program of the year.

Cori: I know. And *to manage the program efficiently, we request the full-time services of a summer intern.*

Christine: Just exactly how much more work will you be taking on?

Cori: ~~Although we have not yet planned how to meet this increased production requirement, we spoke at our last weekly meeting about how we may be inadequately staffed to achieve the performance level expected of our group.~~ This program alone will require four publication projects, Christine. First, the full production—from planning to printing—of the new relocation guidebook, which you requested we produce for international associates.

**FIGURE 4-11** CONT.
**CHECKING FOR THE SUPPORT**

Christine:  How long should this production take?

Monica:  Jillian, as senior associate, you'd be assigned to the planning phase. How long should that take?

Jillian:  **We expect planning of this book alone to take four weeks of my full-time effort. Add to that time two weeks for completing a draft of the book.**

Carlos:  Can we outsource it?

Monica:  Sure we can, but **hiring a consulting firm to produce the book according to our needs would cost eighteen thousand dollars, not including my time in overseeing the firm's work. The best production time commitment we've received is six weeks. So we won't gain any time, add a significant cost, and possibly lose control of the project.**

Christine:  All right. What are the other three projects, Cori?

Cori:  **Second, Monica and I tabulated seventeen major revisions to the employee handbook. We'll have to create these revisions with the cooperation of three of our corporate branches: Corporate, Compliance, and Human Resources.**

Carlos:  **Our support should help you tremendously. We can give you all the text for any changes related to employee benefits or employee conduct policies and procedures.**

Monica:  That's great, Carlos, and **Corporate should also work efficiently with us,** thanks to Christine's commitment to this program. But **an experienced associate from our group— maybe Cori—will have to accommodate Compliance with what we expect to be numerous requests for clarification and additional details. Because of Compliance's legal requirements, keeping this department on our schedule should prove especially time consuming.**

Christine:  Okay. What's third?

Cori:  **Third, we have to research, design, and publish the orientation program book, which includes three new sec-**

**FIGURE 4-11** CONT.
**CHECKING FOR THE SUPPORT**

tions: a program agenda, the speakers' biographies, and a corporate directory. Most of the time here is in developing content and designing a fresh look. Creative time, as you know is the lengthiest. **We can assign our two other associates, Frank Temple and Jessica Garial, to this project, which may take two weeks.**

Monica: **That rounds out all our staff.**

Cori: And fourth, **we have to integrate the program's PowerPoint viewgraphs into the annual "Snapshots from the Program" booklet.**

Christine: Do we really need that booklet?

Monica: No. **Instead of publishing it, we can forgo a uniform look and ask all the presenters to submit their PowerPoint viewgraphs two weeks before the program. Then we can photocopy and staple them as a set and insert them in the new hires' folders for distribution on the first day of the program. We don't need anything fancy here. But this should save us only several hours of coordination time, as we traditionally have produced this booklet from our desktop. The lion's share of the creative development and production time is in the three other publications.**

Christine: Can we do without any of these publications for the orientation program?

Cori: ~~Your interesting and indisputable point during that meeting—that we should impress our new hires with an efficient orientation process was an excellent one that I believe surpasses all other matters~~. These publications have proven to be useful to our new associates, who have consistently given them high ratings on the program evaluation forms. *This is why hiring an intern may be a solution to our problem.*

Christine: Well, that's important to us.

Cori: That's for sure.

Christine: What would the intern actually do for the group?

**FIGURE 4-11 CONT.**
**CHECKING FOR THE SUPPORT**

Cori: *During our orientation season, from May 29 through August 17, an intern would be able to help with a variety of functions, including the development of training manuals, duplication of materials, research of training resources on the Internet, distribution of materials, creation of a new associate database, and coverage on our main phone line.* This would free up Jillian to compose the relocation guidebook, me to manage the employee hand-book, and Frank and Jessica to focus on the orientation program book.

Christine: This seems like a reasonable request.

Carlos: Would you want me to develop a list of candidates for the position?

Cori: Yeah. That would be great. Especially any candidates from the local colleges. *It may be possible to look into recruiting one from either New York College or City Academy. This may offer the additional benefit of opening relations with the placement offices of these two colleges.*

Christine: Good idea. How much would we pay?

Cori: *In checking with Human Resources, I learned that the Company's standard intern rate is $15 per hour.* Assuming twenty percent administrative overhead for the 11-week period, the intern would cost us approximately $8,000, *which seems to be well within our budget.*

Monica: Should we follow the regular employee screening process?

Cori: *If the Publications Unit receives management approval to hire the summer intern by March 28, Jillian, can you begin interviewing applicants from the Human Resources candidate bank by April 18 and select three final candidates for management approval by April 25?*

Jillian: I'd be happy to.

Christine: Sounds good. Go for it.

Cori: Thanks, Christine. ~~Publications~~ *I appreciate the opportunity to present this proposal, and I am prepared to assist in the decision making process, if needed.*

Figure 4-12 shows how her new draft, accounting for *support*, would look. Three of its new problems are:

· lengthy content

- long paragraphs
- inconsistent style, shifting from formal to informal

However, the third element of the 4S Plan—structure—should take care of these first two matters, and the fourth element—style—should deal with the final one.

## FIGURE 4-12
## THE SUPPORT—THIRD OF FIVE DRAFTS

**To:** Monica Ruiz
**From:** Cori Parlin
**Date:** February 8, 2005
**Subject:** Request for a Summer Intern

Human Resources has requested that our unit provide training material for its new-hire orientation program, when the Company will process approximately 150 recently graduated new employees. To manage the program efficiently, the Publications Unit requests the full-time services of a summer intern.

The new-hire orientation program will require four new publications, which have proven to be useful to our new associates, who have given them consistently high ratings on the program evaluation forms. Publications can modify one of these to save time, but the other three will require intensive effort by our staff and the need for increased help.

We can possibly improve production efficiency with the annual "Snapshots from the Program" booklet, by forgoing its uniform look and working directly from the presenters' PowerPoint viewgraphs two weeks before the program. Then we can photocopy and staple them as a set and insert them in the new hires' folders for distribution on the first day of the program.

However, this should save us only several hours of coordination time, as we traditionally have produced this booklet from our desktop. The lion's share of the creative development and production time is in the three other publications.

The first of these is the full production—from planning to printing—of the new relocation guidebook, which Christine Ross requested that we produce for international associates. Jillian Weinstein, our senior associate, estimates planning of this book to take four weeks of full-time effort and two weeks for completing a draft of the book. Outsourcing this project in the interest of improv-

**FIGURE 4-12** CONT.
**THE SUPPORT—THIRD OF FIVE DRAFTS**

ing internal production commitments is a possibility, but hiring a consulting firm to produce the book according to our needs would cost eighteen thousand dollars and a substantial amount of management's time to oversee the firm's work. The best production time commitment we've received is six weeks. So we won't gain any time, we'll add a significant cost, and possibly lose control of the project.

The second production is the new edition of the employee handbook, for which we have tabulated seventeen major revisions. We'll have to create these revisions with the cooperation of three of our corporate branches: Corporate, Compliance, and Human Resources. Corporate should work efficiently with us, thanks to Christine Ross's commitment to this program. Human Resources should also help tremendously by giving us all the text for any changes related to employee benefits or employee conduct policies and procedures. However, I will be assigned to accommodate Compliance with what should be numerous requests for clarification and additional details. Because of Compliance's legal requirements, keeping this department on our schedule should prove especially time consuming.

Third, we have to research, design, and publish the orientation program book, which includes three new sections: a program agenda, the speakers' biographies, and a corporate directory. Most of the time here is in developing content and designing a fresh look. Two other associates, Frank Temple and Jessica Garial, will work on this project, which may take two weeks.

With our entire staff assigned to this project, hiring an intern may be a solution to our problem. During our orientation season, from May 31 through August 19, an intern would be able to help in a variety of functions, including the development of training manuals, duplication of materials, research of training resources on the Internet, distribution of materials, creation of a new associate database, and coverage on our main phone line. This would free up Jillian to compose the relocation guidebook, me to manage the employee handbook, and Frank and Jessica to focus on the orientation program book.

It may be possible to look into recruiting one from either New York College or City Academy. This may also offer the additional benefit of opening relations with the placement offices of these two colleges. Jillian has mentioned that she would be happy to supervise the intern's work. In checking with Human Resources, I learned that the Company's standard intern rate is $15 per hour. Assuming twenty percent

## Structure

The *structure* builds the purpose *statement* and *supporting* details in a logical and clear way to help the reader process the information. The three key elements of the structure are *organization, paragraphing,* and *format.* A well-planned document would probably need little revising for structure, especially after the writer took the time to work on its statement and support. In fact, you can take care of multiple revising issues simultaneously. But for now, let's take a look at them one at a time.

### Organization—The ODC

We want our readers to get a big picture view of our document from the moment they pick it up. They will want to find the opening, the discussion, and the closing (ODC) of our document, and they will want to see the point where the opening gives way to the discussion, as well as the point where the discussion gives way to the closing. For most memos, letters, and lengthier e-mail, the basic elements of the ODC are:

*Opening:* · a purpose statement ←──────────────────┐
       · a preview of the content to follow, if helpful ←──┐ │
*Discussion:* · the supporting details             │ │
*Closing:* · a review or summary of the content discussed ─┘ │
       · the next steps, or call to action ─────────────┘

We already saw how the next steps directly relate to the purpose; in the same way, the review relates to the preview. The letter in Figure 4-13 shows all the elements of the ODC.

# FIGURE 4-13
## THE OPENING-DISCUSSION-CLOSING

**Opening**

December 21, 2004

Ms. Carol Roberts, Chief Financial Officer
Mega Omega Corporation
800 Centennial Avenue
Piscataway, New Jersey 08854

Dear Ms. Roberts:

[ Purpose ]

This letter and its three attachments provide you with some of the financial information you requested to help you prepare for your annual internal fiscal audit kickoff
meeting scheduled for February 11. Below I highlight the key points to consider
concerning the attachments, and I note the pending statement you can expect from us
after the year's end.

[ Preview ]

**Discussion**

**Attachment 1: Statement of Earnings**
We computed the net earnings per share by dividing net earnings by the weighted
average number of common shares outstanding.

**Attachment 2: Balance Sheet**
The total common shareholders' equity includes four factors:
· all common stock at $1 par value, which totaled 406 million shares
· paid-in capital
· retained earnings
· accumulated other comprehensive income

**Attachment 3: Statement of Cash Flow**
New operating activities impacting on cash flow include environmental remediation
charges and merger integration costs.

**Pending Attachment: Statement of Common Shareholders' Equity**
We will complete the fourth statement, your Consolidated Statement of Common
Shareholders' Equity, as soon as we receive year-end common stock values and your
common stock cash dividend distribution statement. Assuming we will have received
these figures by December 31, we will complete the statement for your review by
January 6, 2005.

[ Support ]

**Closing**

I trust that you will find this information useful as you deploy your audit team for its
important engagement. If you need more information or need clarification on any of the
new categories, please call or e-mail me. We look forward to assisting you during the
audit process in any way we can.

[ Review ]

Sincerely,

[ Next Steps ]

Robert Rivera
Vice-president

## Paragraphing

Every paragraph should have a main point, and every sentence in the same paragraph should directly relate to that point. In other words, effective paragraphing shows its *IQ*—its main *idea* at the top and its *qualifiers* following it:

*Idea:*           The main point, the big idea, the topic sentence of the paragraph; the statement that the paragraph makes.

*Qualification:* The details of the paragraph; the support of the main point, usually by *restricting, elaborating,* or *illustrating* it:

- The qualifying sentences *restrict* the meaning of the idea when they limit its definition.

- The qualifying sentences *elaborate* on the meaning of the idea when they provide reasons for or additional details about it.

- The qualifying sentences *illustrate* the meaning of the idea when they give one or multiple examples of it.

Below are examples of qualifying the idea by restriction, elaboration, and illustration:

IDEA—RESTRICTION
The first sentence contains the big idea of the paragraph, and the following sentences restrict the meaning of the idea by limiting its definition. In the example paragraph in Figure 4-14, the idea of the company's success is restricted by the single qualification of sales growth.

## FIGURE 4-14
## IDEA—RESTRICTION

**Idea—Restriction**  The company expects a year of record-breaking success. Worldwide sales should increase by 33 percent, spurred primarily by the global installation of our innovative online client services. For the fourth consecutive year, company-wide sales have outpaced industry figures by double digits. We have good reason to believe that this trend will continue, as orders for our knowledge-management software are bound to remain among the highest in the technology-support product category. This will especially be the case in our Latin American and Pacific-rim markets, where the demand for developing management skills leads the world.

## IDEA—ELABORATION

The first sentence contains the big idea of the paragraph, and the following sentences elaborate on the meaning of the idea by providing reasons for it. In the example in Figure 4-15, the idea that the company should relocate its plant is elaborated by three reasons.

**FIGURE 4-15**
**IDEA—ELABORATION**

| | |
|---|---|
| Idea—<br>Elaboration | Our recommendation that the company relocate its New York City plant to Edison, New Jersey, emerges from comprehensive analysis of three critical factors. First, the $11 per-square-foot difference between the two facilities will enable the company to recover its moving expenses within three months and to realize overhead savings of 11 percent annually thereafter. Second, the additional 7,000 square feet of space in the Edison facility offers our company immediate expansion opportunities. Third, according to several surveys and reports, the labor pool for technical specialists required by our company is 50 percent greater in Central New Jersey than in our present location. |

## IDEA—ILLUSTRATION

The first sentence contains the big idea of the paragraph, and the following sentences support the meaning of the idea with one or multiple examples. In the example in Figure 4-16, the idea that the research and development team is diverse and experienced is illustrated by three examples.

**FIGURE 4-16**
**IDEA—ILLUSTRATION**

| | |
|---|---|
| Idea—<br>Illustration | Our 11-member Research and Development Team is as diverse as it is experienced. We originate from 9 nations on 5 continents and have education or employment credentials from 29 nations and territories on all 7 continents. All of us have post-graduate degrees, two in physics, three in chemistry, four in biology, and two in environmental engineering. We have led or supported multi-national, multi-year, and multi-million dollar research projects in the fields of agronomy, bionics, cryogenics, genetics, hydroponics, molecular physics, nuclear physics, oceanography, oncology, radiology, seismology, and telecommunications. |

### Format

When revising your document, consider using *headings* and *bullets* or *numbers* where you can separate and highlight key points.

Use **headings** when separating more than one idea supporting the purpose. For instance, if you have three reasons for recommending a course of action, you may use the headings:

*Reason 1: Affordability*
*Reason 2: Productivity*
*Reason 3: Quality*

These headings will guide your readers through the content and serve as helpful reference markers if they return to the document. The five principles for using headings are:

- relevance
- consistency
- brevity
- specificity
- order

RELEVANCE. Headings divide all the supporting ideas that are relevant to the purpose. Example:

**Purpose:**   To introduce a recently appointed director
**Headings:** Relevant Experience
              New Responsibilities
              Company Goals

CONSISTENCY. Headings should be conceptually equal, or parallel, in form. Example:

| Parallel Headings | Nonparallel Headings |
|---|---|
| Principle One | One Principle |
| Principle Two | The Second Principle |
| Principle Three | Principle Three |

BREVITY. Headings should be as brief as possible without sacrificing their value to the reader. Example:

| Effective Headings | Ineffective Headings |
|---|---|
| Problem | The Problem Addressed |
| Method | Our Method |
| Solution | The Solution to the Problem |

SPECIFICITY. Headings should preview their content. Example:

| <u>Effective Heading Preview</u> | <u>Ineffective Heading Preview</u> |
|---|---|
| **Project X** | **Project X** |
| Selma discussed the team's progress with Project X. She noted that Phase 2 is complete, and she scheduled the completion of the third and final phase of the project for October 12, two months ahead of schedule because of additional research help from Michele Fineman, the new research analyst. | Selma discussed the team's progress with Project X. She noted that Phase 2 is complete, and she scheduled the completion of the third and final phase of the project for October 12, two months ahead of schedule because of additional research help. |
| **New Staff** | Mike introduced Michele Fineman to the team. She has joined us from the Investment Research Group and will be our Research Analyst. Her first assignment is to support Selma as a researcher on Project X. |
| Mike introduced Michele Fineman to the team. She has joined us from the Investment Research Group and will be our Research Analyst. | |

ORDER. Headings should appear in a logical order based on the reader's concerns. Example:

| <u>Effective Order of Headings</u> | <u>Ineffective Order of Headings</u> |
|---|---|
| Problem | Problem |
| Background | Option A |
| Methodology | Option B |
| Option A | Discussion |
| Option B | Background |
| Discussion | Methodology |
| Recommendation: Option A | Recommendation: Option A |

If headings separate the big ideas of a document, then **numbers** or **bullets** separate items within a big idea. Bullets and numbers provide an effective means of targeting the key information about an idea, and they eliminate the need for wordy transitional phrases.

Careful writers distinguish between bullets and numbers. Although they should carefully organize either, writers send a different message to readers when using one or the other.

NUMBERS. Number a list for any of three reasons: to show priority, sequence, or reference.

| Reason | Description | Example |
|--------|-------------|---------|
| Priority | To show that the order has a particular significance (e.g., rank, importance). | Our four investment options, in order of preference, are as follows:<br>1. mutual funds<br>2. common stocks<br>3. government bonds<br>4. commodities futures |
| Sequence | To show a chronological order of events. | The user must perform three steps:<br>1. Print all working drafts.<br>2. Back-up the hard drive.<br>3. Power-down the system. |
| Reference | To refer to the items at another point in the document. | We should relocate the company for two reasons:<br>1. to save on the cost of office space<br>2. to expand our talent pool selection<br><br>Reason 1 will serve our corporate short-term objectives and Reason 2 our long-term objectives. |

BULLETS. Bullet a list for one reason only: to show equality among the listed points. In the example below, the writer's use of bullets implies that the order of the points is unimportant.

We selected Ms. Obando as the office manager for her three key assets:

- her 12 years of managerial experience
- her outstanding communication skills
- her positive attitude toward our strategic initiative

THE RULE OF SIX. The Rule of Six is a helpful principle to guide you in formatting your documents. It addresses information overload by guiding the writer—and ultimately the reader—to manage the flow of information. Though not to be taken literally in every writing situation, the rule states that writers should limit to six their headings per level, bullets or numbers per list, or lines per paragraph. The following examples show how the Rule of Six applies.

## Headings

In Version 1, the writer treats all 26 ideas as equal, making for a challenging reading task.

**VERSION 1**
Problem: Present Word Processing Software
Examples of Problem
Impact of Problem
Solution: Purchase New Word Processing Software
Method: Review Option A and Option B
Features of Option A
Endorsements of Option A
Cost of Option A
Usability of Option A
System Compatibility of Option A
Technical Support for Option A
Upgrades for Option A
Advantages of Option A
Disadvantages of Option A
Features of Option B
Endorsements of Option B
Cost of Option B
Usability of Option B
System Compatibility of Option B
Technical Support for Option B
Upgrades for Option B
Advantages of Option B
Disadvantages of Option B
Conclusion: Option A Is Better for Our Company
Recommendation 1: Trial Purchase of Option A for Executive Office
Recommendation 2: Develop Training Module for Using Option A

In Version 2, the writer regroups the 26 ideas using levels of heading. Reader ease increases dramatically. Especially notice four points:

1. By comparing Option A and Option B side-by-side, the writer eliminates the need for Advantages and Disadvantages sections for each option.
2. By grouping with subheadings, the writer better establishes relationships among the selling points of each option.
3. The writer discovers opportunities for adding new levels of heading (i.e., national and local sources and convenience).

4. No level of heading exceeds the threshold number of six.

**VERSION 2**
PROBLEM: PRESENT WORD PROCESSING SOFTWARE
    Examples of Problem
    Impact of Problem
SOLUTION: PURCHASE NEW WORD PROCESSING SOFTWARE
METHOD: REVIEW OPTION A AND OPTION B
OPTION A AND OPTION B
    Endorsements
        <u>National Level (Magazines, Surveys)</u>
            *Option A*
            *Option B*
        <u>Local Level (Clients, Vendors, Staff)</u>
            *Option A*
            *Option B*
    Usability
        <u>Features</u>
            *Option A*
            *Option B*
        <u>Compatibility</u>
            *Option A*
            *Option B*
        <u>Convenience</u>
            *Option A*
            *Option B*
    Technical Support
            *Option A*
            *Option B*
    Cost
        <u>Purchase</u>
            *Option A*
            *Option B*
        <u>Upgrades</u>
            *Option A*
            *Option B*
CONCLUSION: Option A Is Better for Our Company
RECOMMENDATIONS
        1. Trial Purchase of Option A for Executive Office
        2. Develop Training Module for Using Option A

## Bullets

In Version 1 on page 116, the writer lists 10 bullet points as equal. This practice defeats the purpose of bullets, namely, to help the reader process essential information.

**VERSION 1**

The following think tanks cover education issues:

- Brookings Institution
- Cato Institute
- Center for Education Reform
- Education Policy Institute
- Education Industry Group
- Heartland Institute
- Heritage Foundation
- Hoover Institution
- Hudson Institute
- Program on Educational Policy and Governance

In Version 2, the writer regroups the 10 bullet points into two sections to help the reader better process the essential information. Notice how the Rule of Six applies.

**VERSION 2**

The following think tanks cover education issues only:

- Center for Education Reform
- Education Policy Institute
- Education Industry Group
- Program on Educational Policy and Governance

The think tanks below cover education issues as well, but they also cover a broad range of public policy issues:

- Brookings Institution
- Cato Institute
- Heartland Institute
- Heritage Foundation
- Hoover Institution
- Hudson Institute

## Paragraphs

Effective paragraphs easily can run more than six lines, and ineffective paragraphs can run fewer than six. Therefore, well-written paragraphs need no line limit. Nevertheless, remembering the six-line paragraph rule helps the writer—and ultimately the reader—manage the flow of information. In Version 1 on page 117, the writer has packed far too much important information in one paragraph.

**VERSION 1**

I thoroughly reviewed with Ms. Pepper her submitted sample and worked with her on a live document concerning goals and metrics for her production department. During the month that I worked with her, she called me twice at my office to help her edit brief documents that she was completing. I covered several teaching points with her. One was creating consistently labeled "working titles" for each paragraph or section of her draft to keep her content focused. Another point was using bullets in parallel form to achieve conciseness and target the reader's needs. I also worked with her on reaching the primary reader (e.g., immediate supervisor) with sufficient completeness to support the needs of a potential secondary reader (e.g., divisional vice-president). All of these points are intended to give her writing more emphasis, coherence, and unity in single-point, well-developed paragraphs.

In Version 2, the writer applies the six-line rule. Notice the five important revisions that the writer makes for clarity and conciseness:

1. Separates the paragraph's two big ideas: the review process and the teaching points.
2. Moves up the last sentence to support the first sentence of the second paragraph.
3. Edits the word to describe the number of teaching points from *several* to *three*.
4. Uses bullets to list the three teaching points.
5. Eliminates the transitional phrases "one was," "another point was," and "I also worked with her on," which are no longer necessary in bullet format.

**VERSION 2**

I thoroughly reviewed with Ms. Pepper her submitted sample and worked with her on a live document concerning goals and metrics for her production department. During the month that I worked with her, she called me twice at my office to help her edit brief documents that she was completing.

To give her writing more emphasis, coherence, and unity in single-point, well-developed paragraphs, I covered with her three teaching points:

- creating consistently labeled "working titles" for each paragraph or section of her draft to keep her content focused
- using bullets in parallel form to achieve conciseness and target the reader's needs
- reaching the primary reader (e.g., immediate supervisor) with sufficient completeness to support the needs of a potential secondary reader (e.g., divisional vice-president)

# FIGURE 4-17
## THE STRUCTURE—FOURTH OF FIVE DRAFTS

**Date:**   Friday, May 6, 2005, 3:07 p.m. EDT
**To:**   Myra Schreiber, Manager
**From:**   Bobby Aldomori
**Re:**   Recommendation for Weekly IT Team Meeting
**CC:**   Jason Jeffers, Manager, Information Technology Team

In an effort to improve our client service and create a seamless working relationship with the Information Technology Team, I propose a weekly meeting with our group and IT. Below are a summary of our and IT's recent service problems and how a weekly meeting would address those problems.

PROBLEM
As you know, our server has crashed three times in the past month, preventing us from making the necessary changes to our website in a timely manner. This has created three problems:

1. Two of our clients, Eastern Focus and North Star Industries, have complained about receiving outdated information.
2. Our three web designers were idle for between two and three hours during each of these incidents.
3. The IT Team has had to delay by a week the installation of its new anti-virus software installation package.

PROPOSED SOLUTION
I believe that IT is committed to providing us with consistently integrated, prompt, and effective troubleshooting services. By holding a weekly status meeting with IT, we can create and regularly review a checklist covering all pending troubleshooting efforts and planned server updates.

Meetings should not run more than a half hour, and we can hold them at 8:00 a.m. before everyone's normal business rush hours, or at another mutually convenient time. Only the manager and an associate representing each group on a rotating basis would need to attend. They should be sufficient to keep the teams abreast of the latest IT developments affecting their group.

BENEFITS
This meeting should result in providing significant benefits to our group and to IT:

- We would provide more reliable and prompt responses to our clients' requests for information.
- We would experience less downtime.
- Our group and IT would enjoy a better working relationship by sharing common concerns and meeting regularly on a professional level.
- IT associates would grow their reputation for client service and eventually free up a lot of their troubleshooting time through good planning and preventive maintenance.

NEXT STEPS
To begin this process, I would create an IT checklist that lists our common IT problems and checkpoints. In addition, I would set up a meeting with Jason Jeffers to plan the first weekly meeting.

I suggest that we make this proposal an agenda item during our next production meeting on Wednesday, and I would be willing to make any modifications that you recommend prior to the meeting. I look forward to discussing this possibility with you, and I appreciate your consideration.

Let's see how Bobby and Cori use structure to improve their documents by employing the organization, paragraphing, and formatting tips provided on the previous pages. First, compare Figure 4-10 with Figure 4-17 below to see how Bobby approached structural improvements to his document. To make his proposal more readable, Bobby makes seven changes:

*Opening-Discussion-Closing*

1. He adds a preview sentence: "Below are a summary of our and IT's recent service problems and how a weekly meeting would address those problems."
2. He adds more content to the closing.
3. He clearly separates the opening from the discussion, and the discussion from the closing.

*Paragraphing*

4. He separates the lengthy proposed solution paragraph into two paragraphs, each with a distinct idea.

*Format*

5. He uses headings for easy reader reference.
6. He uses numbers to list the problems and in doing so, discovers three discrete ones.
7. He adds bullets to make the key benefits stand out and to enable his reader to compare the problems with the benefits.

Now, compare Figure 4-12 with Figure 4-18 to see how Cori uses *structure* techniques to address her organization problems. Cori makes seven changes:

*Opening-Discussion-Closing*

1. She adds the preview sentence "This memo reviews Publications' projected increased work and how assigning a summer intern to special projects would assure our timely and effective completion of the work."

*Paragraphing*

2. She breaks up lengthy paragraphs at their transition points.
3. She moves up the sentence "This would free up Jillian to compose the relocation guidebook, me to manage the employee handbook, and Frank and Jessica to focus on the orientation

program book" to separate the paragraph content from the bullet list. For practice, see Exercise 4-3 on page 132.

*(Continued on page 122)*

## FIGURE 4-18
## THE STRUCTURE—FOURTH OF FIVE DRAFTS

**To:** Monica Ruiz
**From:** Cori Parlin
**Date:** February 8, 2005
**Subject:** Request for a Summer Intern

Human Resources has requested that our unit provide training material for its new-hire orientation program, when the Company will process approximately 150 recently graduated new employees. To manage the program efficiently, the Publications Unit requests the full-time services of a summer intern. This memo reviews Publications' projected increased work and shows how assigning a summer intern to special projects would assure our timely and effective completion of the work.

PROJECTING THE WORK
The new-hire orientation program will require four new publications, which have proven to be useful to our associates, who consistently have given them high ratings on the program evaluation forms. Publications can modify one of these to save time, but the other three will require intensive effort by our staff and create the need for increased help. A description of the four publication projects and our approach to them appears below.

*Snapshots of the Program*
We can possibly improve production efficiency with the annual "Snapshots from the Program" booklet by forgoing its uniform look and working directly from the presenters' PowerPoint viewgraphs two weeks before the program. Then we can photocopy and staple them as a set and insert them in the new hires' folders for distribution on the first day of the program.

However, this should save us only several hours of coordination time, as we traditionally have produced this booklet from our desktop. The lion's share of the creative development and production time is in the three other publications.

*New Relocation Guidebook*
The first of these is the full production—from planning to printing—of the new relocation guidebook, which Christine Ross requested that we produce for international associates. Jillian Weinstein, our senior associate, estimates planning of this book to take four weeks of full-time effort and two weeks for completing a draft of the book.

Outsourcing this project in the interest of improving internal production commitments is a possibility, but hiring a consulting firm to produce the book according to our needs would cost eighteen thousand dollars and a substantial amount of management's time to oversee the firm's work. The best production time commitment we've received is six weeks. So we would not gain any time, we would add a significant cost, and possibly lose control of the project.

*Employee Handbook—New Edition*
The second production is the new edition of the employee handbook, for which we have

**FIGURE 4-18** cont.
## THE STRUCTURE—FOURTH OF FIVE DRAFTS

tabulated seventeen major revisions. We'll have to create these revisions with the cooperation of three of our corporate branches: Corporate, Compliance, and Human Resources. Corporate should work efficiently with us, thanks to Christine Ross's commitment to this program. Human Resources should also help tremendously by giving us all the text for any changes related to employee benefits or employee conduct policies and procedures.

However, I will be assigned to accommodate Compliance with what should be numerous requests for clarification and additional details. Because of Compliance's legal requirements, keeping this department on our schedule should prove especially time consuming.

*Orientation Program Book*
Third, we have to research, design, and publish the orientation program book, which includes three new sections: a program agenda, the speakers' biographies, and a corporate directory. Most of the time here is in developing content and designing a fresh look. Two other associates, Frank Temple and Jessica Garial, will work on this project, which may take two weeks.

EMPLOYING AN INTERN
With our entire staff assigned to this project, hiring an intern may be a solution to our problem. This would free up Jillian to compose the relocation guidebook, me to manage the employee handbook, and Frank and Jessica to focus on the orientation program book.

*Assignments*
During our orientation season, from May 31 through August 19, an intern would be able to help in a variety of functions, including:

- typing training manuals
- photocopying materials
- researching training resources on the Internet
- distributing materials
- creating a new associate database
- covering our main phone line

*Recruitment*
It may be possible to look into recruiting one from either New York College or City Academy. This may also offer the additional benefit of opening relations with the placement offices of these two colleges.

*Supervision*
Jillian has mentioned that she would be happy to supervise the intern's work.

*Salary*
In checking with Human Resources, I learned that the Company's standard intern rate is $15 per hour. Assuming twenty percent administrative overhead for the 11-week period, the intern would cost us approximately $8,000, which seems to be well within our budget.

If the Publications Unit receives management approval to hire the summer intern by March 28, Jillian can begin interviewing applicants from the Human Resources candidate bank by April 18 and select three final candidates for management approval by April 25. I appreciate the opportunity to present this proposal, and I am prepared to assist in the decision-making process, if needed.

*Format*

4. She divides the center into two main headings.
5. She divides each heading into logical subheadings for easy reader reference.
6. She adds a lead-in sentence for the four work projects: "A description on the four publication projects and our approach to them appear below."
7. She uses bullets to list the possible functions of an intern.

## Style

The final element of the 4S Plan in revising is *style*:

- The *statement* is the document manager.
- The *support* is the document material.
- The *structure* is the document builder.
- The *style* is the document artist.

*Style* is the particular sense that the writer gives the reader: personal or impersonal, general or technical, informal or formal. It is also the way that the writer dresses up the document to reinforce the statement. Here we concern ourselves with the *context* language that should accompany the *content* language (the *support*), including transition words and phrases. Figure 4-19 shows how awful our documents would "sound" without the right *style*.

### FIGURE 4-19
### STYLE—BALANCING *CONTENT* LANGUAGE
### AND *CONTEXT* LANGUAGE
*(Context language is italicized.)*

| Content Language Only | Content Language with Context Language |
|---|---|
| You have been promoted. | *We are pleased to inform you that* you have been promoted. |
| We must terminate your services. | *We are sorry that* we have to discontinue our working relationship. |
| Enclosed is the material you requested. | *Thank you for requesting information about our product.* We *are happy to* provide the enclosed material *to help you in deciding whether to use our services.* |
| If necessary, call me. | *If you have any question or need more information about our services, please* call me. |

Context language also shows up in our transition words and phrases. Like signposts on a road, transitions help the reader connect ideas in a document. They are necessary for a host of reasons: cause and effect, comparison and contrast, and sequence, among others. If you have ever felt thrown off the track in the middle of a document, the writer might have failed to provide a helpful transition. Figure 4-20 lists some transitions.

## FIGURE 4-20
## TRANSITION WORDS AND PHRASES

| Purpose | Examples |
| --- | --- |
| Cause | accordingly, as a result, because, consequently, hence, since, so, then, therefore, thus, to this end |
| Comparison | again, also, compared with, in the same way, likewise, once more, similarly |
| Contrast | although, but, despite, even though, however, in contrast, in spite of, instead, nevertheless, nonetheless, notwithstanding, on the contrary, on the one hand...on the other hand, regardless, still, though, yet |
| Concession | admittedly, although it is true that, granted that, it may appear that, of course, while...is true |
| Conclusion | as a result, as we have seen, in any event, in conclusion, in short, on the whole, therefore, to summarize, clearly |
| Emphasis | as you can see, as you know, clearly, indeed, of course, surely, to clarify, undoubtedly |
| Example | after all, even, for example, for instance, in fact, specifically, such as, the following example, to illustrate |
| Place | above, adjacent to, below, beyond, closer to, elsewhere, far, farther on, here, near, nearby, opposite to, there, to the left, to the right |
| Repetition | again, as has been noted, as we have seen, as mentioned earlier |
| Sequence | again, also, and, and then, besides, finally, first...second...third..., furthermore, last, moreover, next, still, too |
| Summary | as a result, as we have seen, clearly, in any event, in conclusion, in other words, in short, on the whole, therefore, to summarize |
| Time | after a while, afterward, as soon as, at last, at length, at that time, before, currently, earlier, immediately, in the meantime, in the past, lately, later, meanwhile, now, presently, shortly, simultaneously, since, so far, soon, subsequently, then, thereafter, until, when |

How much context language is too much? That entirely depends on the purpose of your document and your relationship with the readers. Technical writers, for instance, want their user manuals to be as impersonal as possible; salespeople, on the other hand, prefer a more personal approach when writing a sales letter.

Bobby and Cori decide to make further revisions in their fifth draft to adjust their style. They see a need to tighten their balance of *content* and *context* language by adding or deleting transition words and phrases. From a careful reading of their changes in Figures 4-21 and 4-22, you will infer that some of their revisions are practical and others political. Added words are underlined and deleted words are crossed out.

For practice, see Exercise 4-4 on pages 133–134.

## FIGURE 4-21
## THE STYLE—FIFTH OF FIVE DRAFTS

**Date:** Friday, May 6, 2005, 3:07 p.m. EDT
**To:** Myra Schreiber, Manager
**From:** Bobby Aldomori
**Re:** Recommendation for Weekly IT Team Meeting
**CC:** Jason Jeffers, Manager, Information Technology Team

~~In an effort~~ to improve our client service and create a seamless working relationship with the Information Technology Team, I propose a weekly meeting with our group and IT. Below ~~are a summary of~~ I summarize our and IT's recent service problems and suggest how a weekly meeting would address those problems.

PROBLEM
~~As you know,~~ our server has crashed three times in the past month, preventing us from making the necessary changes to our website in a timely manner. This has created three problems:

1. Two of our clients, Eastern Focus and North Star Industries, have complained about receiving outdated information.
2. Our three web designers were idle for between two and three hours during each of these incidents.
3. The IT Team has had to delay by a week the installation of its new anti-virus software installation package.

PROPOSED SOLUTION
~~I believe that~~ IT is committed to providing us with consistently integrated, prompt, and effective troubleshooting services. By holding a weekly status meeting with IT, we can create and regularly review a checklist covering all pending troubleshooting efforts and planned server updates.

Meetings should not run more than a half hour, and we can hold them at 8:00 a.m. before everyone's normal business rush hours, or at another mutually convenient time. Only the

FIGURE 4-21 CONT.
## THE STYLE—FIFTH OF FIVE DRAFTS

manager and an associate representing each group on a rotating basis would need to attend. They should be sufficient to keep the teams abreast of the latest IT developments affecting their group.

BENEFITS

This meeting should result in providing <u>four</u> significant benefits to our group and to IT:

- We would provide more reliable and prompt responses to our clients' requests for information.
- We would experience less downtime.
- ~~Our group~~ <u>We</u> and IT would enjoy a better working relationship by sharing common concerns and meeting regularly ~~on a professional level~~.
- IT associates would grow their reputation for client service and eventually free ~~up a lot of~~ their troubleshooting time through ~~good planning and~~ preventive maintenance.

NEXT STEPS

To begin this process, I would create an IT checklist that lists our common IT problems and checkpoints. In addition, I would set up a meeting with Jason Jeffers to plan the first weekly meeting.

I suggest that we make this proposal an agenda item during our next production meeting on Wednesday, and I would be willing to make any modifications that you recommend prior to the meeting. I look forward to discussing this possibility with you, and I appreciate your consideration.

## FIGURE 4-22
## THE STYLE—FIFTH OF FIVE DRAFTS

**To:**     Monica Ruiz
**From:**   Cori Parlin
**Date:**   February 8, 2005
**Subject:**  Request for a Summer Intern

Human Resources has requested that our unit provide training material for its new-hire orientation program, when the Company will process approximately 150 recently graduated new employees. To manage the program efficiently, the Publications Unit requests the full-time services of a summer intern. This memo reviews Publications' projected increased work and shows how assigning a summer intern to special projects would assure ~~our~~ timely and effective completion of the work.

PROJECTING THE WORK

The new-hire orientation program will require four new publications, which have proven to be useful to our associates, who consistently have given them high ratings on the program evaluation forms. Publications can modify one of these to save time, but the other three will

# FIGURE 4-22 CONT.
# THE STYLE—FIFTH OF FIVE DRAFTS

require intensive effort by ~~our~~ staff and create the need for increased help. A description of the four publication projects and ~~our~~ Publications' approach to them appears below.

*Snapshots of the Program*

We can ~~possibly~~ improve production efficiency with the annual "Snapshots from the Program" booklet by forgoing its uniform look and working directly from the presenters' PowerPoint viewgraphs two weeks before the program. Then we can photocopy and staple them as a set and insert them in the new hires' folders for distribution on the first day of the program.

However, this should save us only several hours of coordination time, as we traditionally have produced this booklet from our desktop. The lion's share of the creative development and production time is in the three other publications.

*New Relocation Guidebook*

~~The first of these is the~~ This publication requires full production—from planning to printing. ~~of the new relocation guidebook, which Christine Ross requested that we produce for international associates.~~ Jillian Weinstein, our senior associate, estimates planning of this book to take four weeks of full-time effort and two weeks for completing a draft of the book.

Outsourcing this project in the interest of improving internal production commitments is a possibility, but hiring a consulting firm to produce the book according to our needs would cost ~~eighteen thousand dollars~~ $18,000 and a substantial amount of management's time to oversee the firm's work. The best production time commitment we've received is six weeks. So we won't gain any time, we'll add a significant cost, and possibly lose control of the project.

*Employee Handbook—New Edition*

The ~~second~~ third production is the new edition of the employee handbook, for which we have tabulated ~~seventeen~~ 17 major revisions. We'll have to create these revisions with the cooperation of three of our corporate branches, ~~: Corporate, Compliance, and Human Resources. Corporate should work efficiently with us, thanks to Christine Ross's commitment to this program. Human Resources should also help tremendously by giving us all the text for any changes related to employee benefits or employee conduct policies and procedures.~~ one of which is Compliance.

~~However,~~ I will be assigned to accommodate Compliance with what should be numerous requests for clarification and additional details. Because of Compliance's legal requirements, keeping this department on our schedule should prove especially time consuming.

*Orientation Program Book*

~~Third,~~ The fourth production is the orientation program book, which we have to research, design, and publish. ~~the orientation program book, which~~ This book includes three new sections: a program agenda, the speakers' biographies, and a corporate

**FIGURE 4-22** CONT.

## THE STYLE—FIFTH OF FIVE DRAFTS

directory. Most of the <u>production</u> time ~~here~~ is in developing content and designing a fresh look. Two other associates, Frank Temple and Jessica Garial, will work on this project, which may take two weeks.

EMPLOYING AN INTERN

With our entire staff assigned to this project, hiring an intern may be a solution to our problem. This would free up Jillian to compose the relocation guidebook, me to manage the employee handbook, and Frank and Jessica to focus on the orientation program book.

*Assignments*

During our orientation season, from May 31 through August 19, an intern would be able to help in a variety of functions, including:

- typing training manuals
- photocopying materials
- researching training resources on the Internet
- distributing materials
- creating a new associate database
- covering our main phone line

*Recruitment*

~~It may be possible to look into recruiting one~~ <u>We may recruit an intern</u> from either New York College or City Academy. This may also offer the additional benefit of opening relations with the placement offices of these two colleges.

*Supervision*

Jillian has mentioned that she would be ~~happy~~ <u>willing</u> to supervise the intern's work.

*Salary*

~~In checking with~~ Human Resources <u>has informed me</u> ~~, I learned~~ that the Company's standard intern rate is $15 per hour. Assuming twenty percent administrative overhead for the 11-week period, the intern would cost us approximately $8,000~~, which seems to be well within our budget.~~

If the Publications Unit receives management approval to hire the summer intern by March 28, Jillian can begin interviewing applicants from the Human Resources candidate bank by April 18 and select three final candidates for management approval by April 25. I appreciate the opportunity to present this proposal, and I am prepared to assist in the decision-making process~~, if needed.~~

## Summary

Revising is the first phase of Quality Controlling, Step 3 of the PDQ writing process. It offers writers the chance to use the 4S Plan and attend to their *statement, support, structure,* and *style*. When reviewing their *statement,* they check for a clear *purpose* and *next steps*; when reviewing their *support,* they check that they address their *reader's concerns* related to the purpose; when reviewing their *structure,* they check for organization, paragraphing, and format; and when reviewing their *style,* they check for the appropriate balance of *content* and *context* language by including transition words and phrases.

# EXERCISE 4-1
## CREATING A PURPOSE STATEMENT AND NEXT STEPS

*The e-mails below lack a purpose statement that speaks for the entire message, and next steps that provide a clear course of action. Write a purpose statement and next steps for each. Possible solutions appear at the end of the chapter.*

SAMPLE A

| | |
|---|---|
| Re: | Trade Fair |
| Date: | 1:11 p.m. EST 2005-3-25 |
| From: | CarsonCollins@anywhere.com (Carson Collins) |
| To: | Pat@anywhere.com (Pat Tap) |

Pat,

I have a question about setting up our display at the trade fair in Houston. How much space will the convention center give us?

I will need the King story boards from your office so that I can ship them to Houston before we get there.

Thanks,
Carson

Purpose Statement?

_____

_____

_____

_____

Next Steps?

_____

_____

_____

_____

**CONTINUE ON NEXT PAGE**

**SAMPLE B**

| | |
|---|---|
| Re: | Assignment |
| Date: | 1:35 p.m. EST 2005-3-25 |
| From: | CarsonCollins@anywhere.com (Carson Collins) |
| To: | Pat@anywhere.com (Pat Tap) |

Pat,

You asked me to remind you of our next meeting on Tuesday, March 29, in Conference Room B, 109 West Avenue. Are the annual reports going to be ready by then? Kim Kittle, whom we hired last week, needs to have her employee ID activated. Last Thursday, I began my new assignment on the Leigh Project and believe that I can revise the due date to April 29.

Thanks,
Carson

**Purpose Statement?**

_____

_____

_____

_____

**Next Steps?**

_____

_____

_____

_____

## EXERCISE 4-2
## CHECKING THE SUPPORT

*Respond to the e-mail below by answering the reader's questions and giving her more than she asked for. The city to which she is relocating may be any you know well.*

Re:      My Visit to Your City
Date:    3:19 p.m. GMT 05-3-24
To:      Pat@anywhere.com (Pat Tap)
From:    Virginia.Montana@anywhere.com (Virginia Montana)

Hello Pat,

I look forward to attending the new associates conference the week of 18 April at your office. Since I have been based in our offshore annex and have never been to your country, I am wondering whether you could offer some advice concerning my one-week stay. Specifically, I would appreciate answers to the following questions:

· Would you know how far is the Flagship Hotel, where I will stay, from your office?

· Are there any nearby, interesting theatrical productions or art exhibits from 16 April through 22 April?

· Which restaurants would you recommend?

I thank you for your help and hope to meet you at the conference.

Regards,
Virginia

# REVISING FOR STRUCTURE

*Organize and format the memo report below using headings, bullets, and tables. Remember the Rule of Six.*

MEMORANDUM

To:     Rita Reader
From:   Roland Writer
Date:    May 9, 2005
Subject: Recommendation for Purchasing the Handy Lx

In response to your request of May 2, 2005, this memo provides my research on the Handy Ix as a management tool. Upon careful analysis, I believe that the R&D Department should purchase the Handy Lx for our seven researchers and two support staffers because it is a popular, versatile, convenient, and affordable means of meeting our organizing and communicating needs.

With 60 percent of the U.S. market share, the Handy Lx is the leading color handheld communicator, according to *Computing Professional,* which, along with *Electronic World* and *Future Communicator* magazines, recommends it as the premier handheld primarily on the strength of its pervasiveness in the telecommunication, pharmaceutical, investment banking, and environmental engineering industries. In addition, Omni Source and Blue & Green, our two largest clients, and Earthsafe and Lucid, our two largest vendors, use it widely. In fact, three researchers in our Love Creek Office already know how to use the Handy Lx and have reported positive comments about it.

The Handy Lx meets all our portable data processing and communication needs. It can store 16 megabytes of information, and it interfaces with a wide range of software applications, including our current word processing and spreadsheet programs. It includes e-mail capability and is compatible with our e-mail program. In addition, it easily downloads files using any Internet service provider. Besides these features, it stores thousands of appointments, to-do items, memos, and addresses and phone numbers. It also contains a scientific calculator.

The convenience of using a Handy Lx is noteworthy. Its innovative features include pager and cell phone capability, thereby allowing the user to replace a traditional organizer, cell phone, pager, and calculator with this one device. It weighs only 5 ounces and measures 5" long X 3" wide X ¾" thick and has the BeamMeIn technology, which in seconds enables users to exchange selected data with the press of a button. Its Syncho-in-a-Winko cradle, which connects to any of our laptops or desktops, enables users to duplicate data in a separate, secure location, ensuring the preservation of data and offering the user the option of entering data on the handheld or on a personal computer. The user may enter data directly on the Handy Lx by using a stylus on its built-in virtual keyboard or on its RealWrite script screen, which replicates actual handwriting. The Handy Lx runs on two AAA batteries, which generally last 2-3 months, depending on the extent of the user's activity. Users can also visit the Handy website to download updated software and other recently developed support features.

The Handy Lx costs $400, which is $50 less than competing brands whose handhelds do not include telecommunication capabilities. A 10% discount for purchasing over 6 handhelds applies in our case. The cost includes a one-year comprehensive parts and labor warranty.

If you agree with my recommendation that the Handy Lx is an effective, cost-efficient investment for supporting our staff's communicating and organizing needs, I would be pleased to begin the requisitioning process. If you have further questions about the product or would like an in-depth demonstration of it, I will contact a Handy sales representative. Meanwhile, you can visit www.handyandyandmandy.com for additional details. I appreciate your consideration.

# EXERCISE 4-4
## REVISING THE STYLE

SAMPLE A

*Add* context *language to the e-mail below to give the reader a sense of accomplishment and a positive picture of your company.*

Re:       Employment Confirmation

Date:     5:43 p.m. EST 05-3-25

From:     Pat@anywhere.com (Pat Tap)

To:       Gina_Rodda@yourscene.com (Gina Rodda)

Dear Ms. Rodda,

You have been hired by XYZ as an information technology specialist. Your first workday is Monday, April 11. On that day, report at 9:00 a.m. to the Dexter Conference Room at our training facility at 1 King Road for new employee orientation. There you will meet your manager, Tom Schweitzer, who will review your responsibilities.

E-mail me no later than March 31 to confirm that you have accepted your assignment.

Pat Tap

**CONTINUE ON NEXT PAGE**

*Delete context language from the e-mail below to focus the readers on the content they need to know. If necessary, add content.*

Subj:     Training Room Electronic Devices
Date:     2:08 p.m. EST 05-3-28
From:     Pat@anywhere.com (Pat Tap)
To:       Distribution

Team,

Since you asked for directions on what it takes to set up the training room in a proper way that will suit all of you as trainers, I thought I'd give you some neat ideas on the three main things to look for as soon as you enter the room. I think these are the most important things to remember. Here they are:

First, make sure that when you get into the training room, the projection screen moves up and down by flipping the switch. Second, go to the projector remote and ascertain that you can turn it off by remote control without using the main control panel. Finally, see that the monitor has the User ID and Password prompt. Then enter the user ID (trainer) and the password (freedom) on the computer.

As always, sure hope this helps. Let me know if I've forgotten anything. I hope I haven't. You can call me anytime if you think you have any questions, comments, or concerns.

Pat Tap

# SOLUTIONS TO EXERCISES

## EXERCISE 4-1: CREATING A PURPOSE STATEMENT AND NEXT STEPS

Sample A    <u>Purpose Statement</u>:

I need your help with two matters about our display for the trade fair in Houston.

<u>Next Steps</u>:

Please let me know by tomorrow so that I can prepare us for the trade fair.

Sample B    <u>Purpose Statement</u>:

Here are four issues that I promised to follow up with you.

<u>Next Steps</u>:

Please let me know whether you anticipate a problem with any of these issues. I'll see you at the Friday meeting.

## EXERCISE 4-2: CHECKING THE SUPPORT

Re:     Re: My Visit to Your City
Date:   2:46 p.m. EST 05-3-25
From:   Pat@anywhere.com (Pat Tap)
To:     Virginia.Montana@anywhere.com (Virginia Montana)

Hello Virginia,

Here we are all planning an exciting conference for you and the other new associates throughout our regions. I am pleased to answer your questions about your stay in our town.

**Travel from Flagship Hotel**
The Flagship Hotel is a 20-minute ride to the airport and about two miles from our office. Free round-trip transportation by the hotel's shuttle bus from the hotel to our office is available every 30 minutes from 8:00 a.m. to 6:00 p.m. during business days. During off-hours, feel free to travel by taxi and submit a receipt for reimbursement.

**Theater, Art, and Restaurants**
Our city has about ten theaters presenting classical and contemporary dramas and musicals. We have three art museums: the Museum of New Art, which displays world art created after 1900; the City Museum, which features classical sculpture, paintings, and drawings dating from antiquity to the present; and the Museum of American Art, which offers a broad range of art forms exclusively by American-born artists.

The best way to get information of the shows and exhibits that suit your tastes is to visit the following websites, which provide updated information on current presentations:

- www.TheaterinTown.org lists all the theaters in our city, the shows they are running, and brief reviews of the show.
- www.mna.net (Museum of New Art), www.cm.org (City Museum), and www.maa.edu (Museum of American Art) list these museums' current and permanent exhibits.
- Our city has outstanding, affordable restaurants serving most local and ethnic cuisines. Visit www.restaurantsforyou.com and search the cuisine of your choice. If you want to stay within our area, select "midtown."

Virginia, please save your money by not overbooking meals and entertainment. We already have planned for you three great evenings on us:

- On April 16, "Welcome Night," when we will eat at Escargot (French), and see the musical *Les Miserables.*
- On April 18, "New Friends Night," when we will dine at New Orleans (Cajun), followed by a jazz concert at the Philharmonic Hall.
- On April 21, "Bon Voyage Night," when we will bid you farewell with supper at Lemon Grass (Thai), followed by a moonlight boat ride around the city.

I look forward to meeting you and hosting many memorable experiences during your week here.

All the best,
Pat

## EXERCISE 4-3: REVISING FOR STRUCTURE

MEMORANDUM
To:        Rita Reader
From:      Roland Writer
Date:      May 9, 2005
Subject:   Recommendation for Purchasing the Handy I*x*

In response to your request of May 2, 2005, this memo provides my research on the Handy I*x* as a management tool. Upon careful analysis, I believe that the R&D Department should purchase the Handy I*x* for our seven researchers and two support staffers because it is a popular, versatile, convenient, and affordable means of meeting our organizing and communicating needs.

### Popularity
Based on the following information from national and local sources, the Handy I*x* is the leading color handheld communicator.

#### National Sources
*Computing Professional, Electronic World,* and *Future Communicator* magazines recommend the Handy I*x* as the premier handheld because it:
  - commands 60 percent of the U.S. market
  - ranks as the organizer of choice in the telecommunication, pharmaceutical, investment banking, and environmental engineering industries

Local Sources

The Handy Ix already dominates our corporate culture as it is used and preferred by:

- Omni Source and Blue & Green, our two largest clients
- Earthsafe and Lucid, our two largest vendors
- three researchers in our Love Creek Office

## Versatility

The Handy Ix meets all our portable data processing and communication needs—replacing the organizer, cell phone, pager, and calculator—as detailed in the capabilities table below:

| Capability | Features |
|---|---|
| Storage | 16 megabytes memory, up to 25,000 appointments, to-do's, memos, and addresses. |
| Software Interfacing | word processing, spreadsheet, e-mail system |
| Telecommunicating | cell phone, pager |
| Organizing | date book, to-do's, memos, schedulers, address book |
| Downloading | downloads files using any approved ISP |
| Computing | standard scientific calculator |

## Convenience

The Handy Ix offers the user a management tool designed for handling ease, data management and security, power conservation, and quality customer support:

Size

*Weight:* 5 ounces

*Dimensions:* 5" long X 3" wide X ¾" thick

Data

*Inputting:* Three inputting options are available:
- on desktop or laptop
- on handheld using stylus built-in virtual keyboard
- on handheld using the RealWrite script screen, replicating actual handwriting

*Sharing:* BeamMeIn technology, enabling users to exchange selected data in seconds with the press of a button

*Replicating:* Syncho-in-a-Winko cradle, connecting to any laptop or desktop to enable data duplication in a separate, secure location and to ensure data preservation

Power

Two AAA batteries, which generally last 2-3 months, depending on the extent of the user's activity

Handy's website allows users to download updated software and other recently developed support features.

## Affordability

The Handy lx costs $400, which is $50 less than competing brands, whose handhelds do not include telecommunication capabilities. A 10% discount for purchasing over 6 handhelds applies in our case. The cost includes a one-year comprehensive parts and labor warranty.

If you agree with my recommendation that the Handy lx is an effective, cost-efficient investment for supporting our staff's communication and organizing needs, I would be pleased to begin the requisitioning process. If you have further questions about the product or would like an in-depth demonstration of it, I will contact a Handy sales representative. Meanwhile, you can visit www.handyandyandmandy.com for additional details. I appreciate your consideration.

## EXERCISE 4-4: REVISING THE STYLE

## Sample A: Add Context Language

Subj:   Employment Confirmation
Date:   5:43 p.m. EST 05-3-25
From:   Pat@anywhere.com (Pat Tap)
To:     Gina_Rodda@yourscene.com (Gina Rodda)

Dear Ms. Rodda,

Congratulations! On behalf of XYZ, I am pleased to welcome you to our family of committed employees. With this formal offer of employment, we have selected you as an information technology specialist from a large pool of candidates; therefore, you should feel a special sense of accomplishment.

To prepare you for your first day, I have provided some key information below about your first workday:

· We have scheduled your first workday for Monday, April 11.
· At 9:00 a.m., April 11, you will attend new employee orientation at the Dexter Conference Room in our training facility at 1 King Road.
· Sometime that morning, you will meet your manager, Tom Schweitzer, who will review your responsibilities.

So that we may prepare for your arrival, please e-mail me before March 31 to confirm that you have accepted your assignment and that you can begin on your assigned start date. If you have concerns that I have not addressed here, please e-mail me, and I would be happy to respond to you. I wish you well and look forward to meeting you again.

Regards,
Pat Tap

## Sample B: Delete Context Language

Subj:  Training Room Electronic Devices
Date:  2:08 p.m. EST 05-3-28
From:  Pat@anywhere.com (Pat Tap)
To:    Distribution

Team,

Since some of you asked, I summarize below the checkpoints for key electronic devices used in the training room. As you enter the room before a training session:

1.  check the operability of the projection screen switch
2.  test the usability of the projector remote
3.  validate the User ID (trainer) and Password (freedom) prompts

If you have questions about other electronic features in the training room, please let me know and I'll answer them.

Pat Tap

# CHAPTER 5

# Editing

"An editor edits above all to communicate to readers, and least of all to address the sensibilities of editorial colleagues."

– Arthur Plotnik,
*The Elements of Editing*

❧

"We are the products of editing rather than of authorship."

– George Wald, biochemist

❧

"Obviously, where art has it over life is in the matter of editing. Life can be seen to suffer from a drastic lack of editing. It stops too quickly, or else it goes on too long."

– Larry McMurtry, author

This chapter describes the editing phase of Step 3 of the PDQ writing process, and it provides opportunities to practice your hand at your on-the-job editorial skills.

Once writers have determined their purpose *statement*, completeness of their *support*ing details, *structure* of their message, and *style* of writing, they should turn to editing, where they attend to clarity, conciseness, consistency, and correctness of their expression—the sentences, words, punctuation, and mechanics. At this stage of the writing process, writers move from their ideas to the way they state their ideas. Chances are they have spent enough time revising for the issues we saw in Chapter 4 so that they will have little editing to do. This is the case for Bobby and Cori, whose fifth drafts we saw at the conclusion of the last chapter.

The best advice any editor would give to fledgling on-the-job writers is this: "Read your document aloud to hear how it will sound to your reader; if you stumble over your words, so will your reader." If you've *revised* carefully, chances are the idea is fine, but only the expression of the idea is off. Fix it the natural way. Interpret its meaning and restate it as if the reader were sitting in front of you. For example, say you wrote the following sentence:

> As per Jim Armstrong's request, the reason why I am writing this memo is to instruct you as to the proper methodology for installing a DVD drive into your laptop computer.

Most people do not talk like this. How would you actually *say* this to a reader? Probably something like this:

> Jim Armstrong asked that I provide the following instructions for installing a DVD drive in your laptop computer.

Not only does the language sound more natural, but you've reduced the word count from 31 to 18, and you've communicated more directly and clearly to your reader. You do not have to be a grammar expert dissecting sentences to edit documents successfully; you just have to rely on your natural fluency with the spoken word. Editing is no more mysterious than writing it like you would say it.

Nevertheless, in editing mode, you should look at the following issues:

Sentences
- sentence completeness
- parallel structure
- modifier placement
- active-passive voice
- conciseness
- tone

Words
- concrete words
- accurate tense
- pronoun correctness
- pronoun-antecedent agreement
- subject-verb agreement
- word usage mistakes

Punctuation
- end marks
- commas
- semicolons
- colons

- dashes
- parentheses
- hyphens
- apostrophes
- quotation marks
- slashes
- brackets
- ellipses

Mechanics
- numbers
- capitalization
- abbreviations
- spelling

Now let's take these one at a time.

## Sentences

### Sentence Completeness

Complete sentences need a subject and verb, and they express a complete thought. Among the most common problems with complete sentences are *fragments* and *run-ons*.

A *fragment* is a part of a sentence. It does not express a complete thought and cannot stand alone. Examples:

| | |
|---|---|
| *Fragment:* | After the meeting, the deadline was extended. By two days. |
| *Problem:* | The first sentence is fine, but *By two days* is a prepositional phrase that cannot stand alone; therefore, it should be combined with the previous sentence. |
| *Revision:* | After the meeting, the deadline was extended by two days. |

| | |
|---|---|
| *Fragment:* | Working day and night. George completed the newsletter. |
| *Problem:* | *Working day and night* is a participial phrase that modifies George; therefore, it should be combined with the following sentence. |
| *Revision:* | *Working day and night, George completed the newsletter.* |

| *Fragment:* | Marilyn brought her supplies. Pencils, erasers, and note-books. |
|---|---|
| *Problem:* | *Pencils, erasers, and notebooks* is an appositive phrase describing the word *supplies*; therefore, it should be combined with the previous sentence. In this case, use a colon for clarity. |
| *Revision:* | Marilyn brought all her supplies: pencils, erasers, and notebooks. |

A *run-on sentence* is more than one sentence improperly structured as one. Some grammar books treat comma splices separately from run-ons. A comma splice is the inappropriate joining of two complete thoughts with a comma and no connecting word. Because of their similarity, we will treat run-ons and comma splices together. Both express too many thoughts and should be divided into separate sentences, or one part should be subordinate to the other. Examples:

| *Run-on:* | Choosing between the two job candidates is difficult, they are both well qualified. |
|---|---|
| *Problem:* | A comma is insufficient to separate the two complete thoughts. |
| *Revision:* | Choosing between the two well-qualified job candidates is difficult. |
| *Revision:* | Choosing between the two job candidates is difficult *because* they are both well qualified. |
| *Revision:* | Choosing between the two job candidates is difficult; they are both well qualified. |
| | |
| *Run-on:* | In the conference room sat the impatient president and executive staff of White Star Corporation, New York, waiting for the MAR Agency account executive to propose her new advertising campaign, which she promised would move White Star toward a new era of prosperity by merging its technology and wisdom, but she still hadn't arrived without an explanation. |
| *Problem:* | This 57-word sentence has too many connecting clauses and phrases that ramble, causing the reader to lose important meaning. |

*Revision:* In the conference room sat the impatient president and executive staff of White Star Corporation, New York. They were waiting for the MAR Agency account executive to propose her new advertising campaign. She had promised it would move White Star toward a new era of prosperity by merging its technology and wisdom. However, without an explanation, she still hadn't arrived.

For practice, see Exercise 5-1 on page 188.

## Parallel Structure

Parallel structure requires a writer to express parallel thoughts in grammatically parallel terms. Parallel structure achieves word economy and clarifies meaning to help the reader understand complex material. Parallel structure issues usually show up when the word *and* appears in a sentence, and in bullet lists.

*Nonparallel:* Lester enjoys swimming, running, and to hike.

*Parallel:* Lester enjoys swimming, running, and hiking.

*Nonparallel:* The interactive training program is stimulating, a challenge, and offers useful information.

*Parallel:* The interactive training program is stimulating, challenging, and informative.

*Nonparallel:* Please complete the following steps before leaving the office:

1. Have I set the alarm?
2. Lower the heat.
3. The lights must be turned off.
4. Be sure to lock both doors.

*Parallel:* Please complete the following steps before leaving the office:

1. Set the alarm.
2. Lower the heat.
3. Turn off the lights.
4. Lock both doors.

For practice, see Exercise 5-2 on page 189.

## Modifier Placement

Words, clauses, and phrases should be as near as possible to the words they modify. If they drift too far away, they become *misplaced modifiers*, creating an unintended meaning. If they modify nothing at all, they are *dangling modifiers*. Examples:

| | |
|---|---|
| *Misplaced Modifier:* | The trainer asked me occasionally to break during workouts at 15-minute intervals. |
| *Problem:* | Did the trainer *ask* the trainee occasionally or did the trainee *have to break* occasionally? Were the *workout* intervals 15 minutes or were the *breaks* 15 minutes? |
| *Edit:* | The trainer asked me to break occasionally for 15 minutes during workouts. |

| | |
|---|---|
| *Dangling Modifier:* | After raining for ten minutes, I decided to leave the park. |
| *Problem:* | I wasn't raining, although the sentence says that I was. |
| *Edit:* | After it rained for ten minutes, I decided to leave the park. |

For practice, see Exercise 5-3 on page 190.

## Active-Passive Voice

In active voice, the subject acts. *Example:* The manager wrote a proposal.

In passive voice, the subject is acted upon. *Example:* A proposal was written by the manager.

Passive voice uses the verb *to be* (e.g., *be, being, been, am, is, are, was, were*) and a past participle form of a verb.

Passive voice often shows two weaknesses:

1. *a lack of conciseness*
   *Passive:* The report was written by me so that the staff would be informed.
   *Active:* I wrote the report to inform the staff.

2. *a lack of clarity*

    *Passive:*  The payment procedure that is required of new accounts has been reviewed, and it should be printed.

    *Active:*  Publications may print the new account payment procedure that management requires because Accounting has reviewed it.

Convert passive voice to active voice by any of these three methods:

### Method 1

Place the doer before the action.

    *Passive:* The book was read by the attorney.

    *Active:* The attorney read the book.

### Method 2

Change the action to one the subject does.

    *Passive:* My team is composed of two groups.

    *Active:* My team comprises two groups.

### Method 3

Delete the passive verb altogether.

    *Passive:* Be advised that we will close early.

    *Active:* We will close early.

Passive voice may be effective in four cases:

| Reason | Example |
|---|---|
| 1. The doer is clear from the context. | *You are expected to attend the meeting.* |
| 2. The doer is unknown. | *The lost file was returned to my desk.* |
| 3. The doer is unimportant to the meaning. | *The specimen was examined three times.* |
| 4. Reference to the doer is inappropriate. | *Errors were made in the annual report.* |

In the two sample e-mails below, notice the contrasting styles of active and passive voice—and their effect on the reader.

## Passive Voice

Miles,

As was requested by you, this information is being provided about the $100,000 that was deposited by Ms. Miller into a regular statement savings account at the Southchester Branch.

When the account was opened, it was asked whether any capital appreciation objective was intended for these funds, and a no answer was given. An explanation was given about the various money market funds and high-yield corporate bond funds that are offered by the bank, but no interest was expressed. It was pointed out that the customer was in a rush. The account was created within five minutes, and the necessary documentation was given to the customer. Then the customer was wished well.

If more information is needed, an e-mail may be sent.

Sonny

## Active Voice

Miles,

I am providing the information you requested about Ms. Miller's $100,000 deposit into a regular statement savings account at the Southchester Branch.

When Ms. Miller requested that we open this account, I asked whether she had a capital appreciation objective for these funds, and she said, "No." I explained our various money market funds and high-yield corporate bond funds, but she expressed no interest, saying she was in a rush. Within five minutes, I created the account, handed her the necessary documentation, and wished her well.

If you want more information, please e-mail me.

Sonny

Whether we write in active or passive voice is not a right-wrong issue; it is a matter of style. Polished writers know when to use either voice at will, but they prefer active voice as a rule.

For practice, see Exercise 5-4 on page 190.

## Conciseness

Conciseness means making every word count. If a word doesn't add value to your purpose and your reader's concerns, then delete it. Here are five tips for concise writing:

*Conciseness Tip 1: Crunch phrases into words.* Numerous clauses and prepositional phrases can be reduced to single words. Examples:

| Wordy | Concise |
|---|---|
| *Due to the fact that we have limited funds,* we cannot attend. | *Having limited funds,* we cannot attend. |
| *When the company downsizes,* it will reduce staff by 33 percent. | *When downsizing,* the company will reduce staff by 33 percent. |
| Please reschedule the *meeting that was canceled.* | Please reschedule the *canceled meeting.* |
| The book, *which is an antique,* was auctioned for $5,000. | The *antique* book was auctioned for $5,000. |
| Sam is an associate *who can be trusted.* | Sam is a *trustworthy* associate. |
| *In order to be* an effective manager, practice supervising staff. | *To be* an effective manager, practice supervising staff. |
| Marie's desk is *in the office in the corner.* | Marie's desk is *in the corner office.* |
| My *career in telecommunications* spans three decades. | My *telecommunications career* spans three decades. |
| *In the event that* you cannot ignite the pilot light, call the building maintenance department. | *If* you cannot ignite the pilot light, call the building maintenance department. |
| *In light of the fact that* you cannot attend our conference, we will waive the $75 fee. | *Since* you cannot attend our conference, we will waive the $75 fee. |
| *In accordance with your request,* enclosed is a brochure. | *As you requested,* a brochure is enclosed. |
| We should adjust the action plan *at this point in time.* | We should adjust the action plan *now.* |

*Conciseness Tip 2: Remove redundancies.* Redundancies say the same thing twice. Of course, we are aware of the most common ones, but new ones frequently slip into our lexicon. Therefore, we should edit with an eye for the repeated expression. Examples follow.

| | |
|---|---|
| absolutely essential | honest in character |
| advance planning | honest truth |
| and in addition | hot water heater |
| attach together | important essentials |
| basic fundamentals | make an effort to try |
| but nevertheless | mutual benefit to both |
| consensus of opinion | new innovations |
| continues to remain | past experience |
| cooperate together | personal opinion |
| definite guarantee | repeat again |
| depreciate in value | revert back |
| each and every | same exact |
| end result | so as a result |
| expensive in cost | sufficient enough |
| false pretenses | terrible tragedy |
| few in number | top priority |
| final outcome | totally worthless |
| free gift | true facts |
| for the purpose of | unexpected surprise |
| future plans | uniquely one of a kind |
| heavy in weight | various differences |

Below is the world's worst poem. It contains a redundancy on every line—even the title!

> *An Admonishing Warning*
> by Rea Dunn-Dent
>
> A totally perfect writer
> Could show that she's smarter and brighter
> By evading and even escaping
> The trap of repeating and aping
> Words she thinks wise and profound
> But in fact just perplex and confound.

*Conciseness Tip 3: Nix nominalizations.* Sometimes writers transform good verbs into nouns and get stuck using weaker verbs. These phrases, nominalizations, are also known as hidden verbs. This practice deadens the impact of the message. Here are some examples:

| Wordy | Concise |
|---|---|
| take into account | account |
| make an acquisition | acquire |
| arrive at an agreement | agree |
| give approval to | approve |
| have an argument | argue |
| are of the opinion | believe |
| come to a conclusion | conclude |
| take into consideration | consider |
| make a decision | decide |
| place an emphasis on | emphasize |
| conduct an investigation | investigate |
| make a recommendation | recommend |
| put in writing | write |
| serves to suggest | suggests |
| make a effort | try |
| attempt to understand | understand |

*Conciseness Tip 4: Replace rhetorical pronouns.* When the words *it* and *there* have no clear reference, they are used rhetorically, adding words to a sentence. In the examples below, the pronouns *it* and *there* are used as referents, and the sentences are concise:

I brought my laptop but misplaced *it*. (*It* clearly refers to *laptop*.)

Go to an office supply store. You will find permanent markers *there*. (*There* clearly refers to *office supply store*.)

In the next examples, *it* and *there* are used not as referents but rhetorically. Notice how they add words to the sentences:

| Wordy | Concise |
|---|---|
| It is essential that we conclude the investigation. | We must conclude the investigation. |
| It occurred to her that no one had received her reply. | She realized that no one had received her reply. |
| There are three principles guiding our decision. | Three principles guide our decision. |
| He noticed that there wasn't a chair in the office. | He noticed the office had no chair. |

*Conciseness Tip 5: Prefer single-word verbs.* Writers' use of verbs indicates whether their style is business formal. While the phrasal verbs in the left column below seem appropriate for informal e-mails, they lack the conciseness and clarity of the verbs in the right column.

| Avoid | Prefer |
|---|---|
| The issue *boils down* to money. | The issue *becomes* money. |
| Robert will *bring up* the issue. | Robert will *raise* the issue. |
| This report is *broken down* into two parts. | This report is *divided* into two parts. |
| Eben should *come up with* a plan. | Eben should *devise* a plan. |
| I'll call you when I *find out*. | I'll call you when I *know*. |
| John will *get back* to you. | John will *respond* to you. |
| Carol expects *to get by in* math class. | Carol expects *to pass* math class. |
| Paul should *get an idea* of how we work. | Paul should *understand* how we work. |
| I'll *give* Winnie *a call* by Friday. | I'll *call* Winnie by Friday. |
| Raymond may *go ahead* with the project. | Raymond may *proceed* with the project. |
| Camille will *go into* it tomorrow. | Camille will *discuss* it tomorrow. |
| Barbara must *keep in mind* three points. | Barbara must *remember* three points. |
| Please *look out* for problems. | Please *search* for problems. |

| Avoid | Prefer |
|-------|--------|
| Helen asked to *look up* the information. | Helen asked to *research* the information. |
| Elizabeth *put* the meeting *in place*. | Elizabeth *arranged* the meeting. |
| Charles will *put together* the samples. | Charles will *collect* the samples. |
| The writer *rounds out* our creative team. | The writer *complements* our creative team. |
| Anna *seeks out* help when necessary. | Anna *requests* help when necessary. |
| At 11 p.m., we *shut down* the operation. | At 11 p.m., we *terminated* the operation. |
| Claire *took away* a book at the conference. | Claire *took* a book from the conference. |

For practice, see Exercise 5-5 on page 191.

## Tone

More than ever, people from a wide range of industries comment on tone issues cropping up in the writing of their teammates, managers, subordinates, clients, or vendors. When writers "sound" inappropriately critical, comical, or cantankerous, their readers immediately sense the tone problem and begin building emotional barriers between themselves and the content the writers intend to deliver. For most on-the-job situations, the *context* matters as much as the *content*; therefore, the writers' style (*how* they say something) is as important as the message (*what* they say).

Tone problems are simple shifts from an otherwise professional style. You can compare these shifts to visual situations, such as a male executive perfectly groomed and dressed for a client meeting in a power suit, tie, and white shirt—only to be wearing a polka-dot bandana on his head. Or a female director at a board meeting also groomed and dressed in impeccable business-formal attire—except for her multicolored tennis shoes. Obviously, we want to avoid these missteps.

A way to remember seven common tone problems to avoid is through the mnemonic BEMOANS: *bias, egotism, militancy, ostentation, anger, negativity,* and *sarcasm.*

## Bias

Bias appears when a writer indicates or even implies a preference for or an aversion to people or their ideas because of their age, culture, disability, economic status, professional association, race, sex, or sexual orientation. Obvious examples include those in the list below.

| Avoid | Prefer |
|---|---|
| Al's youth affected the project's success. | Al's enthusiasm affected the project's success. |
| Barbara's limited English proficiency precludes her from understanding the new procedure. | Barbara needs more time to learn the new procedure. |
| We selected Charles over Denise because he is more able-bodied. | We selected Charles over Denise because he better meets the requirements of the position. |
| Ed shows sensitivity to his staff unlike most male managers. | Ed shows the sort of sensitivity to his staff expected of good managers. |

Although employees today are aware of most of these instances (i.e., age, culture, disability, economic status, race, sex, or sexual orientation), the *professional association* characteristic might escape them. For instance, the middle manager proposing to senior management the purchase of a new computer system might quote the computer company's advertisement as sufficient proof that it outperforms other brands. Or the equity research writer of an investment-banking firm might tout a favorite stock based solely on past performance while holding similar stocks to a standard derived from sales forecasts and spreadsheet projections. Or the personnel manager might recommend one prospective employee over another to a department head by referring only to the candidate's educational institution.

Corporations hire legal teams to respond to thousands of EEO complaints filed by disgruntled current or former employees or customers. The modern workplace has made diversity and tolerance its *modus operandi*; nevertheless, well-publicized lawsuits leveled against multinational corporations persist. Therefore, it makes sense to check for the myriad ways in which bias surfaces.

## Egotism

Egotistical writing displays a *me* attitude at the expense of *you*—the reader. It favors self-aggrandizement instead of teamwork. This offense to reader awareness and camaraderie emerges in many situations, for instance, in a job candidate's letter of application boasting about his outstanding qualities without showing how his skills would help the company to which he's applying. Or in the sales representative's proposal flaunting her company's outstanding track record to a client whose own particular needs she hasn't even addressed. Or in the office manager's report to the CEO taking complete credit for his team's accomplishments. The list below shows some examples of egotism.

| Avoid | Prefer |
|---|---|
| Your association's honoring my company is further proof that we are industry leaders. | We appreciate your association's generous acknowledgment of our company as an industry leader. |
| I intend to reverse our company's dismal sales performance. | Our organization is determined to improve sales. |
| Without our invaluable assistance, many of our clients would have never improved their production. | We have supported many clients in identifying and correcting production problems, resulting in increased productivity. |
| Since I joined this company two years ago, net income has risen 35 percent. | In the past two years, our team has collaborated to achieve a 35-percent increase in net income. |

Perhaps the subtlest way that egotism manifests itself is not so much by writers bragging about themselves as by the lack of esteem with which they hold their readers. You will often see this occur when subordinates propose a workplace improvement without considering whether their manager has already rejected that option for sound reason. Or when they close their proposal to their manager with a presumptuous "Call me by 3:00 p.m. tomorrow to discuss my ideas further." Writers who check their document for traces of egotism know that to sell their ideas, they must first win over their readers by showing respect for them.

## Militancy

A militant tone denotes a demanding or dictatorial style resulting in a demeaning reader experience. Using aggressive language when a less belligerent approach would do might accomplish the order, but it will also create a hostile work culture. Ultimately, company clients will detect this contentious spirit. The list below offers a few examples of strong-arm tactics.

| Avoid | Prefer |
|---|---|
| You must comply with the policy handbook. | The company expects staff compliance with the policy handbook. |
| I demand a refund of my May 31, 2005, purchase. | I request a refund of my May 31, 2005, purchase. |
| Call me immediately to review your job performance. | Please call me by Wednesday, February 2 to review your job performance. |
| Your efficient execution of our business plan is mandatory. | We appreciate your cooperation in accomplishing our business plan. |

When considering militant language, an awareness of the corporate culture should prevail. Clear directives often must *sound* militant, especially when noncompliance with regulations is not the exception but the rule. And step-by-step instructions written as commands clarify for readers what they must do. Certain organizations even thrive on militant language, so I've heard from officers of military and quasi-military entities (e.g., police, corrections, fire, and sanitation departments). The chain of command and absolute obedience to orders are essential to maintain the culture of discipline. However, this reality does not mean that a police sergeant should transfer that tone when writing a response to an inquiry from a member of the public. Corporate writers should always try to avoid sounding militant for the sake of their organization's *esprit de corps*.

## Ostentation

Ostentation, or pomposity, occurs when writers express ideas designed more to impress readers with their vocabulary than to describe information clearly and concisely. No one finds this practice more obnoxious than readers who have especially strong vocabularies. They see through it as a dilettantish attempt at highbrow affectation. This tone issue frequently plagues writers who face the challenge of moving from a technical to a general style. For instance, investment bankers who regularly write to their industry peers about calls, puts, butterflies, straddles, and strangles need to rethink their jargon when writing to clients untrained in the fine art of futures and options trading. Similarly, engineers should define their terms when writing to non-technical persons about an integrated magnetic media conversion system or a code division multiple access interface.

A far greater abuse of ostentatious writing, however, results from writers succumbing to the temptation of using the latest buzzwords. Once, a client in the telecommunications industry read a memo from a teammate in which the following sentence appeared: "Our organization must leverage economies of scale within the parameters of our production throughputs." Waving the memo in frustration, she exclaimed, "Does anyone really know what that means!" The list below shows additional examples.

| Avoid | Prefer |
|---|---|
| Our organization must leverage economies of scale within the parameters of our production throughputs. | We must manufacture as cost-effectively as our production capacity will permit. |
| Optimal implementation of the report's logistical analysis and forecast is obligatory. | We should fully execute the report's action plan. |
| Louis's obfuscation of the company's reimbursement protocol compelled Michelline to exercise the redundancy option. | Michelline fired Louis because he broke company reimbursement procedures. |
| If assistance can be rendered by this office, contact via e-mail transmission may be effected by the client or authorized representative. | If we can help you, please e-mail us. |

## Anger

Anger shows up when writers are out of control with their emotions—something a reasonable person would admit never works in business. Even if anger achieves limited results in oral communication, we should avoid expressing it in writing because it is irrelevant to the purpose. In other words, while anger might have *inspired* the writing, it is never the *objective* of the document. For instance, a vendor's failure to deliver a critical item on time might anger the customer into writing a letter. However, what the customer really wants is for the vendor to do something—to ship immediately, cancel the order, or compensate him.

The e-mail below presents a classic example of someone with an explosive temper not conducive to moving the business forward who is working in a high-pressure environment.

| | |
|---|---|
| To: | jordanwarden@xyz.com (Jordan Warden) |
| From: | jasonmason@xyz.com (Jason Mason) |
| Date: | 1/25/05 4:32 p.m. EST |
| Re: | January 28 Deadline |

YOU'VE GOT TO BE KIDDING! DON'T YOU UNDERSTAND THAT I'VE GIVEN MCCORMACK MY WORD?! I REFUSE TO ACCEPT EXCUSES. WHY DIDN'T YOU CALL ME BEFORE URSULA LEFT ON HER JUNKET? GET IT DONE AND WITHIN THE BUDGET. DO NOT WRITE AGAIN ABOUT THIS EXCEPT TO CONFIRM THAT YOU'LL GET IT DONE BY JANUARY 28.

&lt;Original Message&gt;

| | |
|---|---|
| To: | jasonmason@xyz.com (Jason Mason) |
| From: | jordanwarden@xyz.com (Jordan Warden) |
| Date: | 1/25/05 1:35 p.m. EST |
| Re: | January 28 Deadline |

Hi, Jason

We have completed the 531 tables of Phase 1 of the Manual Revision Project and are well on our way to completing the 678 figures of Phase 2.

To complete Phase 2 by the January 28 due date, we will need additional help. Ursula Vegbey will be in Houston through the rest of the month at a conference that she had planned to attend before we planned the project. At least 150 of the figures are revisions requiring the hand of a graphic artist, and only Ursula can make them.

Before Ursula left yesterday, she estimated that she would need a week to complete them. If she works through the first weekend of February, would you be able to wait until the morning of February 7 to receive them? If not, what other alternatives do we have?

Jordan

Does Jason really think that screaming will accomplish his meeting the production deadline? If Jason is serious about his deadline—and if he needs Jordan to meet it accurately—he would do everything in his power to support Jordan. If the situation calls for some sort of censure, say, removing Jordan from managing a future project, then Jason should address that matter after completing the project. And, oh, those screaming CAPITAL LETTERS! The e-mail below illustrates how Jason could have written the e-mail if he had sat on his hands before pressing the send button.

To:     jordanwarden@xyz.com (Jordan Warden)
From:   jasonmason@xyz.com (Jason Mason)
Date:   1/25/05 2:08 p.m. EST
Re:     January 31 Deadline

Jordan,

To meet the January 28 deadline, we have three reasonable options:

1.  Recall Ursula from Houston today on an afternoon flight. (I prefer this option.)

2.  Set up the graphic production for this weekend, January 29 and 30, and I will work for Ursula. (I'll do it if Ursula's participation in the conference is more critical to XYZ than meeting this deadline.)

3.  Call Hinton Graphics today and get an immediate quote for on-site production through completion. (I suggest this as a last resort because it will run into no less than $3,000 in production overruns.)

Let me know by 4:30 p.m. today whether Ursula is returning to the office tomorrow or February 1, or if we have to negotiate with Hinton.

Jason

Remembering that the anger expressed in a document remains long after the author's anger has subsided should encourage businesspeople to weed it out of their writing.

### Negativity

Our language—and our culture—is steeped in negativity. Just consider some of our everyday phrases: "don't think twice" (for "be sure of yourself"), "don't hesitate" (for "feel free"), and "don't make a mistake" (for "do it correctly"), among countless others. From the time we were toddlers running around the house in our diapers, we have heard "no no no no no no no."

Now, this is not to criticize Mom and Dad, who told us "no" for our own good; it is simply to state a fact. We are so often told what *not* to do rather than what to do. Think of the first grader who had received a 95 percent on her test, and all Dad wanted to see was the 5 percent she got wrong. Or the third grader whose mother tells him, "Don't make a mess of your room," instead of telling him "Keep your room organized." Peers, teachers, coaches, and employers perpetuate the negativity to the point that it overwhelms our consciousness and becomes second nature to us.

How do we fix it? Simply by choosing the opposite word when editing, as shown in the list below.

| Avoid | Prefer |
|---|---|
| We cannot begin the meeting until Felicia arrives. | We can begin the meeting when Felicia arrives. |
| We reject your proposal because of your high price. | To accept your proposal, we ask that you revise your price. |
| If you have any difficulty, do not hesitate to call me. | If you need help, please call me. |
| Do not worry; I will not disappoint you. | Be sure that I will satisfy your needs. |

Don't forget—er, remember—that you can replace most negatives with positives. As the 1940s song "Don't Let it Bother You" says, "A smile is a frown that's upside down"; whenever a negative word pops up, just turn it upside down.

### Sarcasm

Punctuation is to writing as intonation is to speech; however, we have at our disposal infinitely more inflections in our speech than we have punctuation marks. Punctuation simply cannot compete with the intimacy and immediacy of the voice. For at least this reason, sarcasm does not belong in business correspondence. What may be humorous to one person may be insulting to another. One person's idea of a gag may become incriminating evidence in a class action suit filed by employees charging sex discrimination.

The e-mail below demonstrates just how problematic sarcasm can be. It is an exchange between Karen and Michael, two close friends working for the same organization in different cities. Karen does not tell Mike that she will spend the rest of her workday in a meeting and has asked Jeannie, her administrative assistant, to read and print a copy of Mike's directions and then to forward them to Tanya, an associate who will be flying into Newark on Wednesday as well. Since Jeannie and Tanya do not know the nature of Mike's relationship with Karen, what would they think upon reading his response?

To:      karenoconnor@xyz.com (Karen K. O'Connor)
From:    michaelsilver@xyz.com (Michael T. Silver)
Date:    1/17/05 4:32 p.m. EST
Re:      Directions to the Edison Office

Hey, Karen

Remembering from our Phoenix conference how hopeless you are with directions, I'd better go slowly here. (What was it with you that night, the full moon or the tequila?)

Anyhoo, take the New Jersey Turnpike South (look for the signs this time!) to Exit 10. At the tollbooth, bare right (did I spell that correctly?) and take Route 514 South for one mile and presto—there you are! We're on the right just at the second traffic light you encounter (brief though that encounter may be!!!).

And don't worry: If these directions don't help, nothing will!

Later,
Mike

<Original Message>
To:      michaelsilver@xyz.com (Michael T. Silver)
From:    karenoconnor@xyz.com (Karen K. O'Connor)
Date:    1/17/05 3:07 p.m. CST
Re:      Directions to the Edison Office

Hi Mike,

I'm flying into Newark from Chicago on Wednesday. Would you please give me directions to your office from the airport?

Regards,
Karen

Even if Karen would forgive Mike's feeble and inappropriate attempt at humor, Jeannie and Tanya couldn't help but imagine that Karen and Mike's relationship extends beyond the acceptable norms of business etiquette. The rewrite below shows how Mike should have written the e-mail if he had thought about potential secondary readers, regardless of his relationship with Karen.

To:     karenoconnor@xyz.com (Karen K. O'Connor)
From:   michaelsilver@xyz.com (Michael T. Silver)
Date:   1/17/05 4:32 p.m. EST
Re:     Directions to the Edison Office

Hello, Karen

Here are directions from Newark Airport to our Edison, New Jersey, office at 9630 Woodbridge Avenue.

- Take the New Jersey Turnpike South as you exit the airport.
- Exit at Exit 10.
- Bear right at the tollbooth.
- Take Route 514 South for one mile, where you will see the office on the right just at the second traffic light.

If you need help on the road, call me at 732-777-9876. Enjoy your trip. See you Wednesday.

Regards,
Mike

For practice, see Exercise 5-6 on page 192.

## Words

### Concrete Words

When hearing the word *milk*, you might picture a child drinking from a glass of milk or a hundred cows standing in a barn as their udders are mechanically pumped of milk; similarly, when hearing the word *tree*, you might picture the oak in your backyard or an entire pine forest you visited during your last vacation in the Bavarian mountains.

Many service businesses sell intangibles and, as such, are in fields grounded in abstract language. Consider some of the industry names:

financial services, insurance, intellectual property, investment banking, pharmaceutical research, tax consulting, telecommunications. What do you picture? Certainly nothing as concrete as milking cows or mountain forests.

Communicating is challenging enough without adding to its troubles by riddling messages with jargon and catch phrases peculiar to your field, company, and group. Of course, if the abstract terms are appropriate to your audience, then use them. Abstract words in one context can be concrete words in another context; in fact, using jargon appropriately can save time and actually clarify meaning for your readers. Just be sure that your intended readers cannot misinterpret your words. For practice, see Exercise 5-7 on page 192.

## Correct Tense

In colloquial speech, most of us take great liberties with tense without being misunderstood. We may say, "Holli arrives tomorrow," without worrying about confusing present and future tense because we know our listeners understand us. This sort of speech eventually infiltrates our writing until we confuse our readers, who take written tense more literally. Distinguishing among all the tenses sharpens your editorial pencil. Here is a quick review.

### THE SIMPLE TENSES

| Tense | Singular | Plural |
|---|---|---|
| **Present** *expresses present time* | I see<br>You see<br>He/She/It sees | We see<br>You see<br>They see |
| **Past** *expresses past time* | I saw<br>You saw<br>He/She/It saw | We saw<br>You saw<br>They saw |
| **Future** *expresses future time* | I will see<br>You will see<br>He/She/It will see | We will see<br>You will see<br>They will see |

### THE PERFECT TENSES

| Tense | Singular | Plural |
|---|---|---|
| **Present Perfect** *expresses action started in the past and recently completed or continuing up to the present* | I have seen<br>You have seen<br>He/She/It has seen | We have seen<br>You have seen<br>They have seen |

| Tense | Singular | Plural |
|---|---|---|
| *Past Perfect*<br>*expresses action completed*<br>*before another past action* | I had seen<br>You had seen<br>He/She/It had seen | We had seen<br>You had seen<br>They had seen |
| *Future Perfect*<br>*expresses action that*<br>*will be completed before a*<br>*certain time in the future* | I will have seen<br>You will have seen<br>He/She/It will have seen | We will have seen<br>You will have seen<br>They will have seen |

## THE PROGRESSIVE TENSES

| Tense | Singular | Plural |
|---|---|---|
| *Present Progressive*<br>*expresses action still in*<br>*progress* | I am seeing<br>You are seeing<br>He/She/It is seeing | We are seeing<br>You are seeing<br>They are seeing |
| *Past Progressive*<br>*expresses action in progress*<br>*some time in the past* | I was seeing<br>You were seeing<br>He/She/It was seeing | We were seeing<br>You were seeing<br>They were seeing |
| *Future Progressive*<br>*expresses action in progress*<br>*at some time in the future* | I will be seeing<br>You will be seeing<br>He/She/It will be seeing | We will be seeing<br>You will be seeing<br>They will be seeing |

## THE PERFECT PROGRESSIVE TENSES

| Tense | Singular | Plural |
|---|---|---|
| *Present Perfect Progressive*<br>*expresses action started in the*<br>*past and continuing to*<br>*the present* | I have been seeing<br>You have been seeing<br>He/She/It has been seeing | We have been seeing<br>You have been seeing<br>They have been seeing |
| *Past Perfect Progressive*<br>*expresses continuous action*<br>*completed in the past up to*<br>*another past action* | I had been seeing<br>You had been seeing<br>He/She/It had been seeing | We had been seeing<br>You had been seeing<br>They had been seeing |
| *Future Perfect Progressive*<br>*expresses action that will be*<br>*continuing in the future up to*<br>*a certain time in the future* | I will have been seeing<br>You will have been seeing<br>He/She/It will have been seeing | We will have been seeing<br>You will have been seeing<br>They will have been seeing |

### *Three Common Verb Tense Problems*

Three tense problems surface most often. The correct approach appears in
the list on the next page:

1. Distinguish the past tense with the past perfect tense.

    *Avoid:*   We *had written* the report yesterday.

    *Prefer:*   We *wrote* the report yesterday.

2. Distinguish between the future tense and the present tense.

    *Avoid:*   Oliver *arrives* tomorrow.

    *Prefer:*   Oliver *will arrive* tomorrow.

3. Use past perfect tense when writing about an action that happened in the past but that came before another action that happened in the past.

    *Avoid:*   You *painted* the office before she *occupied* it.

    *Prefer:*   You *had painted* the office before she *occupied* it.

For practice, see Exercise 5-8 on page 193.

## Pronoun Correctness

English grammar contains eight parts of speech: noun, pronoun, verb, adjective, adverb, preposition, conjunction, and interjection. One of the most frequently confused and abused ones is the pronoun. In most situations, all you need to know is the verb of the sentence to determine the proper pronoun. Examples:

| | |
|---|---|
| *Not:* | Lauren and myself go to the convention each year. |
| *But:* | Lauren and I go to the convention each year. |
| *Because:* | *I* go, not *myself* go |

| | |
|---|---|
| *Not:* | Call Christine or myself with questions. |
| *But:* | Call Christine or me with questions. |
| *Because:* | You call *me*, not you call *myself.* |

As you review the pronoun table, note the following tips:

- Nominative pronouns are the subjects, or doers of the action, in a sentence. Examples:

    Linda and *she look* good today.

    *We see* the results.

- Objective pronouns are the objects, or receivers of the action, in a sentence. Examples:

  Parker *talked* to Brenda and *him*.

  The company *hired them*.

- Possessive pronouns are the owners of a noun in a sentence. Examples:

  *Your office* is at the end of the hall.

  *Their property* abuts *ours*.

- Reflexive pronouns reflect back to the subject. Examples:

  *Joe* knows Georgia and *himself*.

  *We* hurt the client and *ourselves*.

## PRONOUNS

| Singular | Nominative | Objective | Possessive | Reflexive |
|---|---|---|---|---|
| *1st Person* | I | me | my, mine | myself |
| *2nd Person* | you | you | your, yours | yourself |
| *3rd Person* | he | him | his | himself |
| | she | her | her, hers | herself |
| | it | it | its | itself |
| | who | whom | whose | |

| Plural | Nominative | Objective | Possessive | Reflexive |
|---|---|---|---|---|
| *1st Person* | we | us | our, ours | ourselves |
| *2nd Person* | you | you | your, yours | yourselves |
| *3rd Person* | they | them | their, theirs | themselves |
| | who | whom | whose | |

When in doubt about which pronoun to use in a series of nouns, remove all the names but the pronoun to hear how the sentence sounds. Examples:

**Paul, Carrie and (I, me, myself) will speak at the seminar.**

*Step 1:*    Remove the nouns in the series: *Paul* and *Carrie*.

*Step 2:*    Try all pronoun options:

   *I* will speak at the seminar.

   *Me* will speak at the seminar.

   *Myself* will speak at the seminar.

*Step 3:*    Select the pronoun that sounds best:

   Paul, Carrie, and *I* will speak at the seminar.

**Send the manual to Paul, Carrie and (I, me, myself).**

*Step 1:*   Remove the nouns in the series: *Paul* and *Carrie*.

*Step 2:*   Try all pronoun options:
Send the manual to *I*.
Send the manual to *me*.
Send the manual to *myself*.

*Step 3:*   Select the pronoun that sounds best:
Send the manual to Paul, Carrie, and *me*.

## Three Helpful Pronoun Rules

1. Use an object pronoun in a prepositional phrase.
   Example: *Between* you and *me*, this job is a challenge for her.

2. Use a nominative pronoun with a linking verb (e.g., *be, being, been, am, is, are, was, were*).
   Example: The problem *is he*. (He is the problem.)

3. When comparing two subjects, keep the case consistent.
   Example: Rita is taller *than she*.

## Who or Whom?

Here's a sure way to decide whether *who* or *whom* is correct:

1. Isolate the phrase following *who* or *whom*.
2. Insert *he/she/they* or *him/her/them* in the selected phrase where it best fits.
3. If *he/she/they* sounds right, use *who*; if *him/her/them* sounds right, use *whom*.

Examples:

| Use ... | Because ... |
|---|---|
| *Who* shall I say is calling? | Shall I say is *he* calling? |
| *Who* did they say was hired? | Did they say *she* was hired? |
| *Who* knows *whom*? | *He* knows *her*. |
| I need *whoever* will help. | *They* will help. |
| I need *whomever* we helped. | We helped *them*. |

For practice, see Exercise 5-9 on page 193.

## Pronoun-Antecedent Agreement

Pronouns should agree in number with their antecedents. The pronouns *anybody, anyone, everybody, everyone, nobody, no one, somebody,* and *someone* are singular and should refer to singular nouns or pronouns. Examples:

| | |
|---|---|
| *Incorrect:* | *Everyone* should have *their* employee handbook. |
| *Correct:* | *Everyone* should have *the* employee handbook. |
| *Correct:* | *Everyone* should have *his* or *her* employee handbook. |
| *Correct:* | *All employees* should have *their* employee handbook. |

| | |
|---|---|
| *Incorrect:* | *Physicians* have a demanding job because *it* is a dynamic field. |
| *Correct:* | *Physicians* have a demanding job because *theirs* is a dynamic field. |
| *Correct:* | *Physicians* have a demanding job because *they* are in a dynamic field. |
| *Correct:* | Physicians have a demanding job because *medicine* is a dynamic *field.* |

For practice, see Exercise 5-10 on page 194.

## Subject-Verb Agreement

Subjects should agree in number with their verbs. Below is a brief discussion of three common mistakes in subject-verb agreement.

*Mistake 1: Misunderstanding pronoun case.* The most common mistake made by writers unfamiliar with subject-verb agreement is in the present tense, third-person singular. Notice in the lists below that only in this case do we add an *s* or *es* to the verb.

SINGULAR

| **Person** | **Past** | **Present** | **Future** |
|---|---|---|---|
| First | I *wrote* | I *write* | I *will write* |
| Second | you *wrote* | you *write* | you *will write* |
| Third | he/she *wrote* | he/she *writes* | he/she *will write* |

PLURAL

| Person | Past | Present | Future |
|--------|------|---------|--------|
| First | we *wrote* | we *write* | we *will write* |
| Second | you *wrote* | you *write* | you *will write* |
| Third | they *wrote* | they *write* | they *will write* |

Therefore, add *s* or *es* to verbs in the present tense, third-person singular, as shown in the examples below:

| Incorrect | Correct |
|-----------|---------|
| he do | he does |
| she know | she knows |
| it look | it looks |

*Mistake 2: Losing agreement in the distance between subject and verb.* Even good editors could overlook agreement when a group of words stands between the subject and the verb. In the example below, the noun clause between the subject (*director*) and verb (*agrees*) functions as an appositive, which adds more information about the subject but is not a part of the main clause; therefore, the subject would not appear in it.

**Incorrect:** The *director*, who has 17 years of experience in running three worldwide divisions for multinational corporations, *agree* with our analysis.

**Correct:** The *director*, who has 17 years of experience in running three worldwide divisions for multinational corporations, *agrees* with our analysis.

In the next example, prepositional phrases, which are never the subject of a sentence, separate the subject (office) and verb (is).

**Incorrect:** The *office* with 16 cubicles and 24 staff members crammed into 900 square feet *are* noisy and unsanitary.

**Correct:** The *office* with 16 cubicles and 24 staff members crammed into 900 square feet *is* noisy and unsanitary.

Therefore, look for the main part of the sentence to determine the subject and verb—and make them agree.

*Mistake 3: Confusing* and *with* or. Using *and* in the subject calls for a plural subject:

> **Incorrect:** *Linda and Masha reviews* Phil's work.
> **Correct:**   *Linda and Masha review* Phil's work.

Using *or* in the subject sometimes calls for a singular or a plural subject:

> **Incorrect:** *Linda or Masha review* Phil's work.
> **Correct:**   *Linda or Masha reviews* Phil's work. (Use singular for one or the other one.)

When *or* separates a singular part of a subject and a plural part, place the plural part closer to the verb and use the plural case.

> **Incorrect:** Linda or Masha's graphic artists reviews Phil's work.
> **Correct:**   Linda or Masha's graphic artists review Phil's work.

For practice, see Exercise 5-11 on page 194.

## Word Usage Mistakes

Many English words have a near-double in appearance or sound with an entirely different meaning. Other word pairs have slightly different meanings. No one promised English would be an easy language, but distinguishing among the words on the list below will make it easier. By the way, the list is a limited one; use your dictionary, grammar book, or dependable online resource to go into greater detail.

### COMMONLY CONFUSED WORDS

| | |
|---|---|
| *a* | Article; use with consonant sounds (e.g., a laptop, a pen, a regulation). |
| *an* | Article; use with vowel sounds (e.g., an easement, an hour, an overview). |
| *accept* | Verb; to receive. (I accept your recommendation.) |
| *except* | Preposition, excluding. (The presentation was outstanding, except for the speaker's bad cough.) |

| | |
|---|---|
| *adapt* | Verb, to change in order to adjust. (The President must adapt to the challenges of a recession.) |
| *adopt* | Verb, to make something one's own. (Will the Congress adopt the President's health care plan?) |
| *advice* | Noun, guidance. (My counselor gave me excellent career advice.) |
| *advise* | Verb, to guide. (My counselor knows how to advise me.) |
| *adverse* | Adjective, unfavorable. (Sailors often contend with adverse conditions.) |
| *averse* | Adjective, disinclined. (The judge is averse to giving a lenient sentence.) |
| *affect* | Verb, to influence. (The firm wants to affect the company's direction.) |
| *affect* | Noun, emotion. (The firm wants to project a human affect in its press releases.) |
| *effect* | Noun, result. (The firm had an effect on the company's direction.) |
| *effect* | Verb, to bring about. (The firm intends to effect a new company policy.) |
| *alot* | Misspelling of *a lot*. |
| *a lot* | Adjective, many. (Clark owns a lot of horses.) |
| *allot* | Verb, apportion. (Vivian will allot her estate among her four daughters.) |
| *allude* | Verb, to make an indirect reference. (Do not allude to the contract talks during the meeting.) |
| *elude* | Verb, to avoid skillfully. (I believe she is trying to elude my question about the contract talks.) |
| *delude* | Verb, to deceive. (Do not delude me into thinking that contract negotiations have been discontinued.) |
| *allusion* | Noun, a reference to something. (The allusion to the firm's founder in your speech inspired me.) |
| *illusion* | Noun, a mistaken idea. (Beware of the illusion that problems will disappear if we ignore them.) |

| | |
|---|---|
| *already* | Adverb, by this time. (Kristen has already mailed the package.) |
| *all ready* | Adjective, prepared. (Our group is all ready for the merger.) |
| *alright* | Misuse of *all right*. |
| *all right* | Adjective, agreeable. (If the resolution is all right, then let's vote on it.) |
| *among* | Preposition, use for more than two. (Share the cash among Tom, Jean, and Keith.) |
| *between* | Preposition, use for two. (Share the cash between Tom and Jean.) |
| *anxious* | Adjective, uneasy, fearful. (Matthew's trembling alerted his audience to how anxious he felt.) |
| *eager* | Adjective, enthusiastic. (I enjoy working with Matthew because he is eager to succeed.) |
| *appraise* | Verb, to set a value on. (The broker will appraise our property tomorrow.) |
| *apprise* | Verb, to inform. (Margaret promised to apprise us of new developments in the case.) |
| *assure* | Verb, to give confidence to. (Bette and Ray assure me that the project will be completed by May.) |
| *ensure* | Verb, to make sure. (Please ensure that Bette and Ray keep their commitment.) |
| *insure* | Verb, to provide insurance. (Should we insure this project for $1 million?) |
| *beside* | Preposition, by the side of. (Gregory stands beside me on this issue.) |
| *besides* | Adverb, furthermore, also. (Besides writing training manuals, Paula is also a corporate trainer.) |
| *bring* | Verb, action toward a point of arrival. (When you come to the meeting, bring your notebook.) |
| *take* | Verb, action from a point of departure. (When you go back to your office, take your notebook.) |

| | |
|---|---|
| *capital* | Noun, an accumulated stock of goods or income. (We need additional capital to build the plant.) |
| *capital* | Noun, a location serving as the seat of its region's government. (The capital of Oregon is Salem.) |
| *capitol* | Noun, a building of the legislature. (The state capitol was built in 1876.) |
| *cite* | Verb, to refer to, to call upon officially. (A researcher must cite sources properly.) |
| *sight* | Noun, something seen. (The Grand Canyon is an amazing sight.) |
| *site* | Noun, location. (The site of our old office building was converted into a parking lot.) |
| *complement* | Noun, complete. (Her impeccable attire is a complement to her professional demeanor.) |
| *complement* | Verb, to complete. (As a team, Gary and Harry complement each other.) |
| *compliment* | Noun, an expression of admiration. (She took my praise as a compliment.) |
| *compliment* | Verb, to express admiration. (We should compliment Barry for his generosity.) |
| *discreet* | Adjective, showing good judgment, unnoticeable. (We remain discreet about client matters.) |
| *discrete* | Adjective, individually distinct. (The logos of two subsidiaries need to be more discrete.) |
| *e.g.* | Adverb, *exempli gratiâ*, from Latin, for example. [I bought the supplies (e.g., pencils, notepads) for class.] |
| *i.e.* | Adverb, *id est*, from Latin, that is. [The U.S. senators from our state (i.e., Prescott and Fitzgerald) attended.] |
| *elicit* | Verb, to bring out. (The ad campaign promises to elicit increased product awareness.) |
| *illicit* | Adjective, unlawful. (The police commissioner said that illicit drug use declined last year.) |

| | |
|---|---|
| *eminent* | Adjective, prominent. (An eminent attorney will address the board of directors.) |
| *imminent* | Adjective, ready to occur. (Last-minute selling in the market suggests that a recession is imminent.) |
| *immanent* | Adjective, universally inherent. (A predisposition toward attaining wealth is not immanent.) |
| *enormity* | Noun, a vicious act. (Congress condemned the terrorist act for its enormity.) |
| *enormousness* | Noun, immenseness. (Sheryl declined to accept the contract because of its enormousness.) |
| *farther* | Adjective, more distant. (Jack lives farther from here than Jill.) |
| *further* | Adjective, extending beyond. (Can we help you further?) |
| *fewer* | Adjective, use with plurals. (Cookie made fewer mistakes than Buster.) |
| *less* | Adjective, use with singulars, for degree, value, amount. (Cookie is less upset than Buster.) |
| *figurative* | Adjective, metaphorical. (The champion held court in his figurative throne—the pressroom.) |
| *literal* | Adjective, factual. (Shelly offered a literal translation of the Japanese allegory.) |
| *flaunt* | Verb, to show off. (Professionals should not flaunt their abilities.) |
| *flout* | Verb, to scorn. (Professionals should not flout the standards set for them.) |
| *good* | Adjective. (Charles wrote a good article.) |
| *good* | Adjective, with linking verb. (Gayle looks good in her suit and feels good about herself.) |
| *well* | Adverb. (Christopher writes well.) |
| *well* | Adjective, for good health. (Connie has felt well since leaving the hospital.) |

| | |
|---|---|
| *grateful* | Adjective, appreciative. (We are grateful for your generous award.) |
| *gratuitous* | Adjective, uncalled for. (His gratuitous criticism embarrassed the staff.) |
| *imply* | Verb, give a hint. (Does my request for a raise imply that I am unhappy?) |
| *infer* | Verb, take a hint. (I infer from my manager's praise that I deserve a raise.) |
| *irregardless* | Misuse of *regardless*. |
| *regardless* | Preposition (used with *of*), without taking into account. (We accept orders regardless of the invoice amount.) |
| *its'* | Misuse of *its* or *it's* |
| *it's* | Contraction of *it is*. (It's three o'clock.) |
| *its* | Possessive pronoun. (Its color is red.) |
| *lay/laid/laid* | Verb, to put or to place. (The gardener will lay the sod today.) |
| *lie/lay/lain* | Verb, to rest or to recline. (Let sleeping dogs lie.) |
| *lead* | Noun, metallic element. (The plumber replaced the lead pipes with plastic tubing.) |
| *lead* | Verb, to guide by going in front of. (Benjamin will lead us through the session.) |
| *led* | Verb, past tense of *lead*. (Benjamin has led us twice during the course.) |
| *orientated* | Misuse of *oriented*. |
| *oriented* | Adjective, to acquaint with a situation. (Harry needs to be oriented to our company's policies.) |
| *passed* | Past tense of *pass*. (Penny passed us on the highway.) |
| *past* | Noun, time gone by. (Chip enjoys reminiscing about his past.) |

| | |
|---|---|
| *premiere* | Noun, first performance. (The premiere of the sitcom will air tonight.) |
| *premier* | Adjective, first in rank. (Compco is our premier client.) |
| *premise* | Noun, proposition. (The scientist's premise for his argument needs clarification.) |
| *premises* | Noun, a building and its grounds. (The maintenance team is charged with cleaning the premises.) |
| *principal* | Noun, chief. (The principal of the company announced a public stock offering.) |
| *principal* | Noun, a capital sum placed at interest. (The principal of the loan is $200,000.) |
| *principal* | Adjective, most important. (Our principal objective is to earn a profit.) |
| *principle* | Noun, a fundamental law or belief. (The right to vote is a principle of democracy.) |
| *stationary* | Adjective, fixed position. (Mavis works out on a stationary bicycle.) |
| *stationery* | Noun, materials for writing. (Crystal has different stationery for every holiday.) |
| *should of* | Misuse of *should have*. |
| *should have* | Auxiliary verb to express obligation. (We should have invested in high-yield municipal bonds.) |
| *than* | Preposition, in comparison with. (Sidney knows Calvin better than Barbara.) |
| *then* | Adverb, at that time. (Barbara knew Calvin better then.) |
| *then* | Noun, that time. (Since then, Sidney and Calvin became acquainted.) |
| *their* | Possessive pronoun. (Their goals are far reaching.) |
| *there* | Noun, that place. (Geri saw Peter standing there.) |
| *they're* | Contraction of *they are*. (They're appealing the verdict.) |

| | |
|---|---|
| *to* | Preposition, movement toward. (Kathy went to the mall.) |
| *too* | Adverb, also, excessive. (Lee too spent too much money.) |
| *two* | Adjective, number. (Lucy owns two boats.) |
| *were* | Verb, plural form of *was*. (Three companies were involved in the lawsuit.) |
| *where* | Noun, what place. (Where did you travel this summer?) |
| *whose* | Possessive pronoun. (Whose book is this?) |
| *who's* | Contraction of *who is*. (Who's attending the Nobel laureate's lecture?) |
| *your* | Possessive pronoun. (Your speech captivated the audience.) |
| *you're* | Contraction of *you are*. (You're due a substantial bonus.) |

For practice, see Exercise 5-12 on page 195.

## Punctuation

As mentioned earlier, punctuation is to writing as intonation is to speech. The best way to determine how to punctuate is to learn the rules, but *listening* for punctuation by reading sentences aloud is a close second. Let the basic rules that follow serve as general guidelines for punctuation, and get used to listening for the placement of punctuation marks. They go a long way toward creating clarity.

## End Marks

| Rule | Example |
|---|---|
| 1. Use a period at the end of a statement. | The first train arrives at noon. |
| 2. Use a question mark at the end of a question. | Does the first train arrive at noon? |
| 3. Use an exclamation mark at the end of an exclamation. | How great that the first train arrives at noon! |

# Commas

| Rule | Example |
|---|---|
| 1. Use a comma before a conjunction (e.g., *for, and, nor, but, or, yet, so*) separating two complete thoughts. | The interviewer asked several thought-provoking questions, and the interviewee responded forthrightly and thoroughly. |
| 2. Use commas to separate items in a series. | We asked for a laptop, digital camera, and PDA. |
| 3. Use commas to enclose nonessential clauses and phrases. | Victor Marsh, who manages our production department, joined the company in 2001. |
| 4. Use commas to enclose interrupters. | You should not assume, Ms. Quincy, that we will be open today. |
| 5. Use a comma to separate introductory clauses and phrases. | Veering off course, the skipper maneuvered the ship through treacherous winds. |
| 6. Use commas to separate items in dates and addresses. | Darius lived at 975 Danger Road, Malta, Montana, from October 10, 1996, to June 6, 2004. |

# Semicolons

| Rule | Example |
|---|---|
| 1. Use a semicolon to separate two complete thoughts not joined by a conjunction, or joined by such words as *accordingly, consequently, for example, furthermore, however, moreover, nevertheless, that is*, and *therefore*. | Ms. Simpson is not in the conference room; she is in her office.

We want to win the contract; however, we do not want to sacrifice our integrity. |
| 2. Use semicolons to separate groups of items in a series using commas. | Running for U.S. President in 1992 were Bill Clinton, Governor of Arkansas; George Bush, President of the U.S.; and Ross Perot, businessman from Texas.

Send the memo to Clifford Perkins, Chief Executive Officer, New York; Molly Kearns, Chief Operating Officer, Chicago; Sam Kendall, Chief Financial Officer, Houston; Perry Winkle, Chief Information Officer, Los Angeles; and Jenny Pepsider, Chief Research Officer, Miami. |

# Colons

| Rule | Example |
|---|---|
| 1. Use a colon to make an announcement, especially after the words *as follows* or *the following*. | We must remember to bring the following tools: hammer, pliers, saw, flat-head screwdriver, and wrench. |
| 2. Use a colon after a salutation in a formal business letter. | Dear Ms. Talbot: |

# Dashes

| Rule | Example |
|---|---|
| Use dashes for dramatic emphasis or to interrupt a thought. | Our investment strategy is to achieve long-term capital appreciation—the same as yours. |
| | Our newsletter reports—exclusively for subscribers—on breaking industry trends. |

# Parentheses

| Rule | Example |
|---|---|
| Use parentheses to enclose parenthetical information. | Senator Cushing (Democrat, New Jersey) threatened to filibuster the defense bill. |
| | Our company has experienced ten years of growth. (See Appendix B.) |
| | Herman bought an antique desk (circa 1892). |

# Hyphens

| Rule | Example |
|---|---|
| 1. Use hyphens to join multi-word modifiers before a noun. | This is a once-in-a-lifetime opportunity for Kenny. |
| 2. Use a hyphen with certain words for clarity. | You have two choices: re-sign or resign. |
| 3. Use a hyphen to join numbers written as words. | twenty-seven, forty-two, seventy-one |
| 4. Use a hyphen to join letters and numbers with the words they modify. | O-ring, T-square, 8-ounce bottle,12-ton ship |

# Apostrophes

| Rule | Example |
|---|---|
| 1. Use an apostrophe to show possession. | Michael's promotion surprised me. |
| 2. Use an apostrophe to contract words. | Toni said she'd write you, but she can't until you're an employee. |
| 3. Use an apostrophe in certain cases for clarity. | Your *h*'s look like *t*'s. |

# Quotation Marks

| Rule | Example |
|---|---|
| 1. Use quotation marks to enclose verbatim quotes. | "This stalemate must be broken," asserted the board member. |
| | "This stalemate," asserted the board member, "must be broken." |
| 2. Use quotation marks to enclose terminology used uniquely in the context of the writing. | Our manager fondly called us "voyagers" because of the innovative research we were conducting. |
| 3. Use quotation marks to enclose titles of reports, articles, essays, short stories, poems, songs, paintings, and other works of art. | While she read the article "How to Winterize Your Summer Home," I read the poem "The Walk in Winter" and the short story "A Deep Freeze." |

# Slashes

| Rule | Example |
|---|---|
| 1. Use slashes in informal writing to separate parts of dates. | Deborah was born 1/29/71. |
| 2. Use a slash to separate a numerator from a denominator in fractions. | We need 48 feet of 1/2-inch copper tubing. |

# Brackets

| Rule | Example |
|---|---|
| Use brackets to enclose the writer's words inserted into a quotation. | The Declaration of Independence states, "All men [and women] are created equal." |

## Ellipses

Rule
Use ellipses to show omission.

Example
In the summer of 1963, President John F. Kennedy told his audience at the Berlin Wall, "When one man is enslaved, no man is free.... All free men, wherever they may live, are citizens of Berlin."

Use ellipses to express random thinking—but never in serious on-the-job writing.

Send a dozen roses to Harriet and wish her a speedy recovery.... Tell Marco I'm still waiting on his blueprints.... Have you seen the galleys of the 2002 annual report?... Are we still on for lunch this Wednesday at the Santorini Café?

For practice, see Exercise 5-13 on page 196.

## Mechanics

*Mechanics* is a term used to denote the nuts and bolts of grammar: those small points that do not fit into the category of grammar or punctuation but still require attention to clarify meaning for the reader. The four areas of mechanics covered here are numbers, capitalization, abbreviations, and spelling.

## Numbers

Technical writers, engineers, and scientists generally express numbers as figures, not as words, because the numbers are their subject matter and need to be plainly visible. Example:

An 8-square-centimeter area of polyvinyl chloride tubing triple-coated with Color R203 exhibited a 75% patina loss when exposed to 1 milliliter of Xylol over a 30-second period.

Some legal writers, on the other hand, persist in expressing numbers both ways, especially when writing contracts. Example:

The tenant will have thirty (30) days to vacate the premises from the date of the eviction notice.

Business writers tend to follow the rules prescribed below:

| Rule | Example |
|---|---|
| 1. Spell out from zero to ten. | Ian read eight books this year. |
| 2. Spell out numbers at the beginning of a sentence. | Fourteen thousand dollars were deposited in the account. |
| (Where practical, work around Rule 2.) | We deposited $14,000 into the account. |
| 3. Spell out approximate numbers. | The catcher, who is in his forties, made over a hundred errors. |
| 4. Spell out one- and two-word ordinal numbers. | This was his thirty-third audition. |
| 5. Spell out fractions standing alone. | The sprinter lost the race by one-hundredth of a second. |
| 6. Spell out numbers before a figure. | The carpenter needs four ½-inch screws. |
| 7. Use figures for numbers more than ten. | You read 11 books this year. |
| 8. Use figures when mixing high and low. | I read 8 books, and you read 11 books. |
| 9. Use figures for ordinal numbers more than two words. | The oldest person in the world celebrated her 121st birthday. |
| 10. Use figures to represent units of time, measurement, or money. | I said, "It's 9 o'clock." She used an 8-ounce cylinder. |

## Capitalization

| Rule | Example |
|---|---|
| 1. Capitalize proper nouns. | City of New York, Research & Development Division |
| 2. Capitalize specific places. | Philadelphia, New Jersey, Indonesia, Eighth Avenue |
| 3. Capitalize geographical regions. | Western New York, Central Canada, Eastern Europe |
| 4. Capitalize names of business products. | Word for Windows, LaserJet |
| 5. Capitalize single letters naming an object. | A-type personality, B-type blood, C-clamp, I-formation, O-ring, S-hook, T-square, X-ray |
| 6. Don't capitalize seasons. | winter, spring, summer, autumn |

# Abbreviations

In formal business writing, abbreviate words sparingly. Federal, state, and municipal governments as well as various industries, such as chemical, pharmaceutical, and telecommunications, have their own abbreviation standards.

## General Abbreviations

| | | | |
|---|---|---|---|
| C.E. | a year in the Common Era (used instead of A.D.) | Mrs. | Mrs. |
| B.C.E. | a year before the Common Era (used instead of B.C.) | Sr. | Senior |
| | | Atty. | Attorney |
| a.m. | *ante meridiem* (before noon) | Dr. | Doctor |
| p.m. | *post meridiem* (after noon) | D.D.S. | Doctor of Dental Surgery |
| Assn. | Association | D.Sc. | Doctor of Science |
| Co. | Company | D.V.M. | Doctor of Veterinary Medicine |
| Corp. | Corporation | Ed.D. | Doctor of Education |
| Inc. | Incorporated | Hon. | Honorable |
| ed. | editor | J.D. | Doctor of Law |
| trans. | translator | M.A. | Master of Arts |
| fig. | figure | M.D. | Doctor of Medicine |
| e.g. | *exempli gratia* (for example) | M.B.A. | Master of Business Administration |
| i.e. | *id est* (that is) | Ph.D. | Doctor of Philosophy |
| etc. | *et cetera* (and so forth) | Prof. | Professor |
| Jr. | Junior | Rev. | Reverend |
| Mr. | Mister | | |
| Ms. | Ms. | | |

## Technical Abbreviations

The abbreviations below are acceptable in technical and scientific writing.

| | | | | | |
|---|---|---|---|---|---|
| amp | ampere | gal | gallon | mL | milliliter |
| bu | bushel | hp | horsepower | mm | millimeter |
| cL | centiliter | hr | hour | min | minute |
| cm | centimeter | in. | inches | oz | ounces |
| dL | deciliter | kg | kilogram | pt | pint |
| dz | dozen | km | kilometer | qt | quart |
| F | Fahrenheit | L | liter | sec | seconds |
| ft | feet | lb | pound | yd | yards |

## United States Postal Service Abbreviations

The following address abbreviations are acceptable on mailing envelopes and in the address lines of letters; however, the words should be spelled out in formal writing.

| | | | | | |
|---|---|---|---|---|---|
| APT | Apartment | AK | Alaska | NE | Nebraska |
| AVE | Avenue | AZ | Arizona | NV | Nevada |
| BLVD | Boulevard | AR | Arkansas | NH | New Hampshire |
| BLDG | Building | CA | California | NJ | New Jersey |
| CTR | Center | CO | Colorado | NM | New Mexico |
| CIR | Circle | CT | Connecticut | NY | New York |
| CT | Court | DE | Delaware | NC | North Carolina |
| DEPT | Department | DC | District of Columbia | ND | North Dakota |
| DR | Drive | FL | Florida | OH | Ohio |
| HTS | Heights | GA | Georgia | OK | Oklahoma |
| JCT | Junction | HI | Hawaii | OR | Oregon |
| LN | Lane | ID | Idaho | PA | Pennsylvania |
| OFC | Office | IL | Illinois | PR | Puerto Rico |
| PKWY | Parkway | IN | Indiana | RI | Rhode Island |
| PH | Penthouse | IA | Iowa | SC | South Carolina |
| PLZ | Plaza | KS | Kansas | SD | South Dakota |
| PT | Point | KY | Kentucky | TN | Tennessee |
| RD | Road | LA | Louisiana | TX | Texas |
| RM | Room | ME | Maine | UT | Utah |
| SQ | Square | MD | Maryland | VT | Vermont |
| STA | Station | MA | Massachusetts | VI | Virgin Islands |
| ST | Street | MI | Michigan | VA | Virginia |
| STE | Suite | MN | Minnesota | WA | Washington |
| TER | Terrace | MS | Mississippi | WV | West Virginia |
| TPKE | Turnpike | MO | Missouri | WI | Wisconsin |
| VW | View | MT | Montana | WY | Wyoming |
| AL | Alabama | | | | |

## Spelling

Now that we have a spell-check feature in our word processors, we don't need to be good spellers, right? Well, not really. Most spellcheckers would not pick up a misspelling of *form* as *from*, *their* as *there*, or many proper names. Searching through books and websites, you can find numerous resources listing the most frequently misspelled words in English. The problem with most of them is this: No matter how many spelling rules they offer, exceptions to the rules usually apply. If you learned to spell exclusively by mastering every spelling rule, you would still stand a strong chance of failing a spelling test. That's how many exceptions you can find.

You probably know many of the rules already. Here are two of the most common ones:

- *i* before *e* (e.g., *brief, piece*) except after *c* (e.g., *receipt, receive*) or when it sounds like *a* (e.g., *freight, weigh*). But *height* is an exception to all that.
- When two vowels go walking, the first one does the talking (e.g., *boat, ease*). But *canoe, eight, enough,* and *through* are among the many exceptions.

Other rules exist—all with enough exceptions to send a poor speller to the dictionary time and again. You can memorize the lists of commonly misspelled words night and day, and this practice will surely help. But nothing replaces reading consciously with an observant eye on the spelling.

For practice on spelling, see Exercise 5-14 on page 197.

## Summary

Editing is the second phase of Quality Controlling, Step 3 of the PDQ writing process. After revising their documents for the clarity and organization of their ideas, writers edit their drafts to ensure that each sentence, phrase, word, and punctuation mark adds value to their purpose. They achieve a well-edited document by checking sentence structure, conciseness, voice, tone, grammar, word usage, punctuation, and mechanics.

# EXERCISE 5-1
## RUN-ONS AND FRAGMENTS

*Correct the fragments and run-ons in the following examples.*

1.  Our Agency thanks you for your decision. To recognize us for our contribution to the business community by naming us an honored guest at your annual luncheon.

2.  Such an acknowledgment validates our advocacy on behalf of small businesses, inspires us to redouble our efforts in ensuring equal access to city government bids.

3.  We gladly accept your invitation to attend the luncheon, our commissioner, Dr. Bonita Oliva, expects to participate.

4.  She wishes to make some appropriate remarks for the occasion. Also requests to know her allotted presentation time.

5.  Dr. Oliva looks forward to enjoying the day's festivities with your company, we wish you well. In planning for a successful event.

# EXERCISE 5-2
## PARALLEL STRUCTURE

*Rewrite these sentences to strengthen their parallel structure.*

1. Cliff contacted the client, wrote the report, and the case was referred.

2. The team succeeds because of their spirit of cooperation, hard work, and they are experts.

3. The manager will need secretarial support, a significant amount of technology, and the commitment of the president.

4. The mover must be careful to perform the following steps:

   1. All information technology equipment requires removal before the general move.

   2. Pack all file cabinet contents into corrugated cartons.

   3. The desks must be disassembled and all hardware must be placed in desk drawers.

   4. Have you covered all chairs in bubble wrap?

   5. Once the floor is empty, the floor should be swept and mopped.

5. We should discuss the following items:

   · The Hickman Project

   · We have had too much staff turnover.

   · Has someone programmed the new laptops?

   · Turn off cell phones and pagers during the meetings.

   · Carla Stein has been promoted to Marketing Director.

# EXERCISE 5-3
## MISPLACED AND DANGLING MODIFIERS

*Check the following sentences for misplaced and dangling modifiers.*

1. In my office, more men lift cartons than women.

2. The hotel built a gym for guests with a sauna.

3. While carrying books, I saw Oscar drop them down the stairs.

4. Since dying, I've noticed that the author's reputation has grown.

5. Traveling through the United States, majestic mountains and breathtaking seashores can be seen.

6. Costing $3 million, our investment group bought the fledgling IPO.

7. Having sent the check yesterday, the vendor still hadn't received the payment.

# EXERCISE 5-4
## PASSIVE TO ACTIVE VOICE; ACTIVE TO PASSIVE VOICE

*Convert the following sentences from passive voice to active voice.*

1. The decision was made to terminate the operation, but several dissenting voices were heard.

2. The accounting group members were visited by the CEO, and they were challenged by him to decide on how operating expenses could be reduced.

3. The software was not requisitioned by Human Resources, so the shipment was disputed by the Accounting Department.

4. If the audit findings have been documented, then the management responses should be written.

*Convert the following sentences from active voice to passive voice.*

5. We will complete the revised draft by March 18, so we suggest that you review it for additional comments by April 1.

6. The company will not renew contracts unless it receives a signature by August 18.

7. Management will suspend members' club privileges if they do not follow the rules.

8. If writers doubt the veracity of a claim, then they should delete it from their manuscript.

# EXERCISE 5-5
## CONCISENESS

*Make the sentences concise without sacrificing their meaning.*

**Crunch phrases into words.**

1. I sent the letter from the manager to the associate, who is new to our company.

2. The packaging equipment that is new should be moved to the area of shipping.

**Remove redundancies.**

3. Past experience portends to tell us that each and every employee should wear an ID badge at this point in time.

4. In my personal opinion, I believe we should reship the package again to the same exact location.

**Nix nominalizations.**

5. Jane will come to a conclusion on the report when you make your recommendation of the product.

6. The committee cannot arrive at an agreement on the study until it finishes conducting its investigation.

**Replace rhetorical pronouns.**

7. It is essential that there be twelve directors at the meeting.

8. It is up to you to decide whether there should be three or four options.

**Prefer single-word verbs.**

9. When we get together, please keep in mind that we can go into only so many topics.

10. If you come up with any new ideas, please get back to me by Friday, and together we'll go over them.

# EXERCISE 5-6
## ELIMINATING TONE PROBLEMS

*Replace these tone issues with people-centered comments.*

1. *Bias:*      The older executives offered great insight into the corporation's mission statement.

2. *Egotism:*    Without my design support, our group would be floundering.

3. *Militancy:*    You must see that our leave policy demands your absolute compliance.

4. *Ostentation:*   I will demonstrate how you can utilize your existing fiscal infrastructure to leverage an adaptive remunerative paradigm.

5. *Anger:*      You have made a poor decision for our organization!

6. *Negativity:*   We do not want to worry about losing this account.

7. *Sarcasm:*    Teri is no Robin Williams when it comes to communicating

# EXERCISE 5-7
## REDUCING ABSTRACT WORDS AND JARGON

*Restate the abstract words and jargon in the sentences below for a general audience.*

1. To effect the requisite outcome of user documentation uniformity, the documenter should submit the penultimate draft to the editorial group for usability testing.

2. Before termination of any operational phase by a shift supervisor, it is recommended that sample lots from the automated conveyor system undergo systematic inspection for any production irregularities.

## EXERCISE 5-8
## VERB TENSE

*Correct the verb tense errors in the troubleshooting report below.*

Last night, Plant Manager Michael Messina runs the Maxwell conveyor at its maximum speed when the belt splits, causing production to be terminating for two hours. Messina explains that the Maxwell sales representative had suggested running the conveyor at maximum speed when production requirements have not been demanding. Such is the case last night.

Messina immediately had followed standard safety procedures at the moment of the incident. No one had been injured. Maxwell will have been contacted since the conveyor was still under warranty. A more comprehensive report on the incident and the resulting lost production costs has been written by tomorrow.

## EXERCISE 5-9
## PRONOUNS

*Select the correct pronoun for the sentences below.*

1.  I enjoyed meeting Bruce and [ **you** • **yourself** ] in Philadelphia.

2.  For people like you and [ **I** • **me** • **myself** ], success comes from effort.

3.  [ **Who** • **Whom** ] did you visit last week?

4.  The house should belong to [ **whoever** • **whomever** ] paid the mortgage.

5.  The house should belong to [ **whoever** • **whomever** ] you bequeathed it.

6.  Nobody writes like Lydia and [ **you** • **yourself** ].

7.  The study went to the officers, Bob, Carol, Ted, and [ **I** • **me** • **myself** ].

8.  Between you and [ **I** • **me** • **myself** ], pronouns drive me crazy.

9.  May's office is roomier than [ **her** • **hers** ].

10. [ **We** • **Us** ] Americans have many privileges.

11. If you have questions, please call Bob or [ **I** • **me** • **myself** ].

12. Cyril wrote the business plan [ **he** • **him** • **himself** ].

# EXERCISE 5-10
## PRONOUN AGREEMENT

*Correct the pronoun-antecedent errors in the sentence below.*

1. A computer scientist must keep abreast of breaking developments in their field.

2. The typewriter is virtually extinct; most writers prefer a computer to them.

3. The company must beware of the challenges to their industry.

4. Josephine's intelligence and diligence will get its just due.

5. Anyone can see for themselves our new product line at the annual trade show.

6. May your determination to be an industry leader never lose their sense of urgency.

7. A salesperson should know when to cut their losses.

# EXERCISE 5-11
## SUBJECT-VERB AGREEMENT

*Correct the ten subject-verb agreement errors in the letter (completely fictitious) below.*

Dear Mr. Columbus,

Ferdinand and I am pleased to underwrite your planned trip to the New World. Our adviser were not in favor of our decision because of the belief that your ships would eventually fall off the planet. Nevertheless, the king remain convinced that your vision and determination is rare, and he want to offer you three ships and a crew for a successful voyage.

We have commissioned the *Niña*, *Pinta*, and *Santa Maria* for your expedition. The *Santa Maria*, which are among the best ships in our fleet, have ample space to house a substantial crew and store enough food for a long excursion. While the *Niña* and *Pinta* is smaller, they consistently receives rave reviews from sailors.

My husband and I, as well as Spain, wishes you a wonderful trip.

Sincerely,
Queen Isabella

# EXERCISE 5-12
## WORD USAGE

*Choose the correct words in the following sentences.*

1. Andrew decided to [**accept** • **except**] [**your** • **you're**] proposal.

2. Barbara's lawyer gave her excellent [**advice** • **advise**].

3. Carlos understands the [**affect** • **effect**] that the raise will have on his lifestyle.

4. Dionne has to [**a lot** • **allot**] too many resources to win the account.

5. Frances distributed the books [**among** • **between**] Amy, Betty, and Cindy.

6. George [**assured** • **ensured**] me that the project would be completed on time.

7. Ken said that an [**eminent** • **imminent**] judge, [**whose** • **who's**] credentials are outstanding, will address the conference.

8. Maury asked to study the data [**farther** • **further**] and wants to know [**were** • **where**] you want the report delivered.

9. Natasha planted [**fewer** • **less**] seeds in the garden this year.

10. Rosemarie's comment about my good work habits [**implies** • **infers**] that I should get a raise.

11. Steve will pay the bill [**irregardless** • **regardless**] of how the work was done.

12. Theresa thinks [**its** • **it's** • **its'**] necessary for us to sign in.

13. Ursula will [**lie** • **lay**] down for a while and rest before her concert.

14. Xavier, as a [**principal** • **principle**] of our company, has strong [**principals** • **principles**] about paying off the loan's [**principal** • **principle**].

15. Yvonne wants [**to** • **too** • **two**] spend [**to** • **too** • **two**] much money for [**to** • **too** • **two**] cars.

# EXERCISE 5-13
# PUNCTUATION

*Punctuate the following sentences.*

1. I wrote e-mail reminders to Mel Thad Dee Dee Sarah and Oliver.

2. The guard cannot however allow us to enter the vault.

3. Carmen has not arrived therefore we should wait for her.

4. Remember this we are seeking one time rights to your manuscript.

5. Attending the conference were Ishmael Garhial Account Executive Minneapolis Enrico Palermo Controller Cincinnati Jeremiah Rogge Marketing Associate Milwaukee and Randi Preston Administrative Assistant Oakland.

6. We are in the Age of Information said Jill Colangelo CEO of TV News Network yet we have never been at greater danger of being misinformed.

7. We need on time deliveries not only now but always.

8. Mark created the procedure and Sonia performed it.

9. Having depleted our budget we cannot make major purchases until the new fiscal year.

10. Please bring with you the following items 3½-inch disks and CD-ROM disks writing pads pens pencils and highlighters and manuals and textbooks.

11. The president accepted all the recommendations of the nominating committee and we decided to implement the action plan immediately.

12. I did not find the memo on the printer I found it on the fax machine.

13. When Mary called the customer claimed that he was shipped the wrong box.

14. Women who rarely entered male dominated professions before the 1970s are now becoming doctors lawyers and executives in increasing numbers.

15. This trainers manuals are in the training room but these trainers manuals are in the conference room.

# EXERCISE 5-14
## NUMBERS, CAPITALIZATION, ABBREVIATIONS, SPELLING

*Treating the memo below as if it were a formal document, correct its errors in mechanics.*

The community improvement committee met on Thur., Feb. 24th '05, from 10AM to 12:15 PM in the chairman's suite. Ms Claudia Nelson led the mtg.

Ms Nelson discussed the new comunity grant applications and had 3 suggestions for improving it: 1st, change the number of reference required from 3 to 2. 2nd let cic review all application changes. 3rd, print the form in times new roman Font.

We discussed grant awards for the Spring cycle. Of the 20000 dollars awarded, 1/2 will go to community care house, 1/4 will go to St John's academy, and the final 1/4 will go to Harris senior homes. Since thirty-two applications were submitted from N.J., Pa., and Oh. during this cycle, our award rate slipped to below ten percent.

46 new applications are being processed for the Summer cycle. We have rejected 17 of these because of insufficient information; 20 were rejected by our Reviewers because of the organizations scope of work and the other nine are finalists. Assuming that we award five applications, we will again exceed our aceptance rate goal of ten pct.

Our next meeting will be on Wed., Mar. 30 in the corp. dining rm.

# Exercise Solutions

## EXERCISE 5-1: RUN-ONS AND FRAGMENTS

1. Our Agency thanks you for your decision to recognize us for our contribution to the business community by naming us an honored guest at your annual luncheon.

2. Such an acknowledgment validates our advocacy on behalf of small businesses and inspires us to redouble our efforts in ensuring equal access to city government bids.

3. We gladly accept your invitation to attend the luncheon. Our commissioner, Dr. Bonita Oliva, expects to participate.

4. She wishes to make some appropriate remarks for the occasion; therefore, she requests to know her allotted presentation time.

5. Dr. Oliva looks forward to enjoying the day's festivities with your company. We wish you well in planning for a successful event.

## EXERCISE 5-2: PARALLEL STRUCTURE

1. Cliff contacted the client, wrote the report, and referred the case.

2. The team succeeds because of their cooperation, diligence, and expertise.

3. The manager will need secretarial support, technological assistance, and presidential commitment.

4. The mover must be careful to perform the following steps:
   1. Remove all information technology equipment before the general move.
   2. Pack all file cabinet contents into corrugated cartons.
   3. Disassemble the desks and place all hardware in desk drawers.
   4. Cover all chairs in bubble wrap.
   5. Sweep and mop the floor once it is empty.

5. We should discuss the following items:
   - the Hickman Project
   - staff turnover
   - programming the new laptops
   - cell phone and pager etiquette
   - Carla Stein's promotion to Marketing Director

## EXERCISE: 5-3: MISPLACED AND DANGLING MODIFIERS

1. In my office, more men than women lift cartons.

2. The hotel built a gym with a sauna for guests.

3. I saw Oscar drop the books he was carrying down the stairs.

4. I've noticed that the author's reputation has grown since his death.

5. Traveling through the United States, we can see majestic mountains and breathtaking seashores.

6. Our investment group bought the fledgling IPO for $3 million.

7. Although the customer sent the check yesterday, the vendor has not received the payment.

## EXERCISE 5-4: PASSIVE TO ACTIVE VOICE; ACTIVE TO PASSIVE VOICE

1. We decided to terminate the operation but heard several dissenting voices.

2. The CEO visited accounting group members and challenged them to decide on how to reduce operating expenses.

3. Human Resources did not requisition the software, so the Accounting Department disputed the shipment.

4. If the auditors document their findings, then management should write its responses.

5. The revised draft will be completed by March 18, so it is suggested that the draft be reviewed for additional comments by April 1.

6. Contracts will not be renewed unless a signature is received by August 18.

7. Members' club privileges will be suspended if the rules are not followed.

8. If the veracity of a claim is doubted, then it should be deleted from the manuscript.

## EXERCISE 5-5: CONCISENESS

1. I sent the manager's letter to the new associate.

2. The new packaging equipment should be moved to the shipping area.

3. Experience tells us that each employee should wear an ID badge now.

4. I believe we should reship the package to the same location.

5. Jane will conclude the report when you recommend the product.

6. The committee cannot agree on the study until it finishes its investigation.

7. Twelve directors must be at the meeting.

8. You should decide whether to offer three or four options.

9. When we meet, please remember that we can cover only a few topics.

10. If you create any new ideas, please e-mail me by Friday, so we can discuss them.

## EXERCISE 5-6: ELIMINATING TONE PROBLEMS

1. *Bias:*      The more experienced executives offered great insight into the corporation's mission statement.

2. *Egotism:*      My design support contributed to our group's successful performance.

3. *Militancy:*      We ask that you comply with our leave policy.

4. *Ostentation:*      I will show how you can use your current resources to develop a flexible salary policy.

5. *Anger:*      Have you considered other options for our organization?

6. *Negativity:*      We want to be sure to satisfy this account.

7. *Sarcasm:*      Teri is a serious communicator.

## EXERCISE 5-7: REDUCING ABSTRACT WORDS AND JARGON

1. To ensure that the instructions are clear and consistent, the writer should send the final draft to the editorial group for review.

2. Before stopping the production line, the shift supervisor should inspect production samples for any quality problems.

## EXERCISE 5-8: VERB TENSE

Last night, Plant Manager Michael Messina was running the Maxwell conveyor at its maximum speed when the belt split, causing production to terminate for two hours. Messina explained that the Maxwell sales representative had suggested running the conveyor at maximum speed when production requirements are not demanding. Such was the case last night.

Messina immediately followed standard safety procedures at the moment of the incident. No one was injured. Maxwell will be contacted since the conveyor is still under warranty. A more comprehensive report on the incident and the resulting lost production costs will be written by tomorrow.

## EXERCISE 5-9: PRONOUNS

1. I enjoyed meeting Bruce and **you** in Philadelphia.

2. For people like you and **me**, success comes from effort.

3. **Whom** did you visit last week?

4. The house should belong to **whoever** paid the mortgage.

5. The house should belong to **whomever** you bequeathed it.

6. Nobody writes like Lydia and **you**.

7. The study went to the officers, Bob, Carol, Ted, and **me**.

8. Between you and **me**, pronouns drive me crazy.

9. May's office is roomier than **hers**.

10. **We** Americans have many privileges.

11. If you have questions, please call Bob or **me**.

12. Cyril wrote the business plan **himself**.

## EXERCISE 5-10: PRONOUN AGREEMENT

1. Computer scientists must keep abreast of breaking developments in their field.

2. The typewriter is virtually extinct; most writers prefer a computer to it.

3. The company must beware of the challenges to its industry.

4. Josephine's intelligence and diligence will get their just due.

5. Consumers can see for themselves our new product line at the annual trade show.

6. May your determination to be an industry leader never lose its sense of urgency.

7. A salesperson should know when to cut his or her losses.

## EXERCISE 5-11: SUBJECT-VERB AGREEMENT

Dear Mr. Columbus,

Ferdinand and I are pleased to underwrite your planned trip to the New World. Our adviser was not in favor of our decision because of the belief that your ships would eventually fall off the planet. Nevertheless, the king remains convinced that your vision and determination are rare, and he wants to offer you three ships and a crew for a successful voyage.

We have commissioned the *Niña*, *Pinta*, and *Santa Maria* for your expedition. The *Santa Maria*, which is among the best ships in our fleet, has ample space to house a substantial crew and store enough food for a long excursion. While the *Niña* and *Pinta* are smaller, they consistently receive rave reviews from sailors.

My husband and I, as well as Spain, wish you a wonderful trip.

Sincerely,

Queen Isabella

## EXERCISE 5-12: WORD USAGE

1.  Andrew decided to **accept your** proposal.

2.  Barbara's lawyer gave her excellent **advice**.

3.  Carlos understands the **effect** that the raise will have on his lifestyle.

4.  Dionne has to **allot** too many resources to win the account.

5.  Frances distributed the books **among** Amy, Betty, and Cindy.

6.  George **assured** me that the project would be completed on time.

7.  Ken said that an **eminent** judge, **whose** credentials are outstanding, will address the conference.

8.  Maury asked to study the data **further** and wants to know **where** you want the report delivered.

9.  Natasha planted **fewer** seeds in the garden this year.

10. Rosemarie's comment about my good work habits **implies** that I should get a raise.

11. Steve will pay the bill **regardless** of how the work was done.

12. Theresa thinks **it's** necessary for us to sign in.

13. Ursula will **lie** down for a while and rest before her concert.

14. Xavier, as a **principal** of our company, has strong **principles** about paying off the loan's **principal**.

15. Yvonne wants **to** spend **too** much money for **two** cars.

## EXERCISE 5-13: PUNCTUATION

1. I wrote e-mail reminders to Mel, Thad, Dee Dee, Sarah, and Oliver.

2. The guard cannot, however, allow us to enter the vault.

3. Carmen has not arrived; therefore, we should wait for her.

4. Remember this: We are seeking one-time rights to your manuscript.

5. Attending the conference were Ishmael Garhial, Account Executive, Minneapolis; Enrico Palermo, Controller, Cincinnati; Jeremiah Rogge, Marketing Associate, Milwaukee; and Randi Preston, Administrative Assistant, Oakland.

6. "We are in the Age of Information," said Jill Colangelo, CEO of TV News Network, "yet we have never been at greater danger of being misinformed."

7. We need on-time deliveries—not only now, but always.

8. Mark created the procedure, and Sonia performed it.

9. Having depleted our budget, we cannot make major purchases until the new fiscal year.

10. Please bring with you the following items: 3½-inch disks and CD-ROM disks; writing pads, pens, pencils, and highlighters; and manuals and textbooks.

11. The president accepted all the recommendations of the nominating committee, and we decided to implement the action plan immediately.

12. I did not find the memo on the printer; I found it on the fax machine.

13. When Mary called, the customer claimed that he was shipped the wrong box.

14. Women, who rarely entered male-dominated professions before the 1970s, are now becoming doctors, lawyers, and executives in increasing numbers.

15. This trainer's manuals are in the training room, but these trainers' manuals are in the conference room.

The Community Improvement Committee (CIC) met on Thursday, February 24, 2005, from 10:00 a.m. to 12:15 p.m. in the Chairman's Suite. Ms. Claudia Nelson led the meeting.

Ms. Nelson discussed the new community grant application and had three suggestions for improving it: first, change the number of references required from three to two; second, let CIC review all application changes; third, print the form in Times New Roman font.

We discussed grant awards for the spring cycle. Of the $20,000 awarded, one-half will go to Community Care House, one-fourth will go to St. John's Academy, and the final one-fourth will go to Harris Senior Homes. Since 32 applications were submitted from New Jersey, Pennsylvania, and Ohio during this cycle, our award rate slipped to below 10 percent.

In all, 46 new applications are being processed for the summer cycle. We have rejected 17 of these because of insufficient information, 20 were rejected by our reviewers because of the organization's scope of work, and the other 9 are finalists. Assuming that we award 5 applications, we will again exceed our acceptance rate goal of 10 percent.

Our next meeting will be on Wednesday, March 30, in the corporate dining room.

# CHAPTER 6

# Proofreading

"One must first correct oneself before correcting others."

— Confucius

❧

"All human errors are impatience, a premature breaking off of methodical procedure."

— Franz Kafka, *Aphorisms*

❧

"I should have no objection to go over the same life from its beginning to the end: requesting only the advantage authors have, of correcting in a second edition the faults of the first."

— Benjamin Franklin

This chapter describes the proofreading phase of Step 3 of the PDQ writing process and provides an exercise to test your proofreading eye.

Now you have written the document, revised it with the 4S Plan in mind, and edited it for accuracy and correctness of expression. As a writer, you have said precisely what you want to say (*statement*), thoroughly addressed your readers' concerns related to your purpose (*support*), detailed all your points in a logical order (*structure*), and checked the way you address your readers (*style*). As an editor, you have checked the document for effective language and correct grammar, usage, and punctuation. But in the process of making a change here and another change there, you might have created new mistakes, so now is the time to print a hard copy and proofread the document.

Yes, one more look at the document. Do not depend solely on the grammar-check and spell-check features of your word processor. These tools are extremely useful but cannot by themselves find every possible error you might have made. Figure 6-1 shows some checkpoints when proofreading. Using this checklist will increase your chances of finding an error everyone else has missed.

Proofreading is an entirely different skill from revising and editing. I've met many people who are not strong writers or editors themselves but have a knack for catching mistakes. Those are the folks you would want to have around to proofread your documents. On the other hand, I have met people who painstakingly—and masterfully—revise and edit their documents, only to weary of the writing task and skip proofreading. You can expect to find in their documents the types of mistakes listed in Figure 6-1.

When proofreading, be sure to use universally accepted proofreading symbols, the most common of which appear in Figure 6-2. In doing so, you can exchange documents with others using a universal correction system. (The printing and publication industries use many more symbols, but the ones in

## FIGURE 6-1
## PROOFREADING CHECKLIST

**Language**
1. Have the names been checked against an accurate original?
2. Have incorrect words that would pass the spell-check feature slipped by (e.g., form/from, field/filed)?
3. Have all pairs been checked (e.g., quotation marks, parentheses, dashes)?
4. Have page transitions been checked for proper continuation of the text?
5. Are the graphics labeled properly?
6. Are the headers and footers consistent with the text?

**Numbers**
7. Are the "continued from" and "continued on" lines correct?
8. Is the date correct?
9. Has the accuracy of all numbers been checked against a correct original?
10. Have number pairs been checked for consistency with each other (e.g., a number referenced in a table and in the text)?
11. Is the pagination correct?

**Print**
12. Are the font type, style, and size consistent in the headings and text?
13. Is the color consistent?
14. Is the print quality consistent?
15. Is the paper free of blemishes?

**Spacing**
16. Is the spacing consistent among the headings, subheadings, and text lines?
17. Is the text free of widows (section or paragraph endings appearing alone at the top of the page)?
18. Is the text free of orphans (section or paragraph beginnings appearing alone at the bottom of the page)?

**Format**
19. Is the alignment correct?
20. Has the table of contents been checked for heading and pagination consistency?
21. Are the graphics set properly?

Figure 6-2 should cover most business and technical writing proofreading situations.)

# FIGURE 6-2
## PROOFREADING SYMBOLS

| Function | Margin Mark | Text Mark |
|---|---|---|
| insert something | ∧ | Because Hank was late, he waited in ∧ office. *the* |
| insert comma | ⌃ | Because Hank was late⌄ he waited in the office. |
| insert apostrophe | ⌄ | Hanks office has a window. |
| insert period | ⊙ | Because Hank was late, he waited in the office⊙ |
| insert question mark | ? | Does Hank's office have a window ? |
| insert exclamation mark | ! | What a view from Hank's office ! |
| insert quotation marks | ⌄⌄ / ⌄⌄ | I said, I like Hank's view. |
| insert colon | ⊙⊙ | I know this for sure⌄ Hank's view is great. |
| insert semicolon | ⌃ | Hank's office is nice⌄ his apartment is even nicer. |
| insert hyphen | ⹀ | Hank's second⌄floor office is new. |
| insert dash | ⊥/M / ⊥/M | Hank's office⌄and only his office⌄is new. |
| insert parentheses | ( / ) | Hank's offices⌄ New York and Chicago⌄ are nice. |
| insert brackets | [ / ] | "I like this office⌄the Chicago one," Hank said, "more than the other one." |
| delete something | ℓ | Hank's office is not in Chicago |
| transpose | (tr) | Hank's is office nice. |
| close up space | ⌣ | Hank's office ⌣is nice. |
| insert space | # | Hank's office⌄is nice. |

**CONTINUED ON NEXT PAGE**

**FIGURE 6-2** CONT.
# PROOFREADING SYMBOLS

| Function | Margin Mark | Text Mark |
|---|---|---|
| begin paragraph | ¶ | Hank's offices are in New York and Chicago. ¶ My office is in Atlanta. |
| no paragraph | No ¶ | Hank's offices are in New York and Chicago. My office is in Atlanta. |
| run in | run in | Hank's offices are in New York and Chicago. |
| capitalize | cap | Hank's offices are in new York and Chicago. |
| lower case | lc | Hank's offices are in NEw York and Chicago. |
| spell out | sp | Hank's offices are in NY and Chicago |
| wrong word | ww | Hank's offices offices are in New York and Chicago. |
| italicize | ital | The Wall Street Journal is in Hank's office. |
| set boldface | bf | Hank Miller, Director of Operations |
| set lightface | lf | Hank's office is nice. |
| wrong font | wf | Hank's offices are in New York and Chicago. |
| align | align | Hank's offices are in New York and Chicago. My office is in Atlanta. |
| let stand | stet | Hank's offices are in New York and Chicago. |
| question to author | ? | Hank's offices are in New York and Houston. Chicago? |

Perhaps people hesitate to proofread because they are not quite sure what proofreading entails, so below is the "Positive Proofreading Procedure," a method for ensuring that your proofreading moves as efficiently, thoroughly, and painlessly as possible. Be sure to use this procedure when your document has to be perfect because it will receive the critical eye of important readers.

## A Positive Proofreading Procedure

### Materials Needed

The main tools needed are a pair of fresh eyes and a hard copy of the document printed on clean, plain, white paper. But the items below will also be useful:

- a ruler for tracking lines of type
- a brightly colored marker to highlight changes
- a magnifying glass for especially fine print
- the Proofreading Checklist (Figure 6-1)
- the list of Proofreading Symbols (Figure 6-2)

### Procedure

**BEFORE YOU PROOFREAD**

1. Allow as much time as you can between the editing and proofreading phases. This will increase your chances of finding more errors.
2. Find a time of day when you are alert and most likely to pick up overlooked errors.
3. Develop a search-and-destroy mentality. Convince yourself that some enemy (actually yourself) has sabotaged your well thought-out manuscript with scores of mistakes, littering your pages with mental land mines designed to distract your readers and kill their interest in your ideas. Resolve to hunt for these one at a time until you have cleared your field of these land mines.
4. Know your typical errors. Are they forgetting to close parentheses and quotation marks, writing *from* as *form* and vice versa,

and allowing spacing and alignment inconsistencies? Assume that you have made such mistakes.

## AS YOU PROOFREAD

5.  Use the ruler starting at the top of the page to isolate lines. (Do not read headers and footers yet; treat them as a separate document to be proofread later.)
6.  Read the words aloud and slowly, pointing at each word as you read it and reminding yourself to read what is in front of you—not what you might think is in front of you.
7.  Use the brightly colored marker to indicate the corrections.
8.  Flag any item you doubt. For instance, if you think that Dr. Page spells her name as Dr. Paige, then highlight the name and verify the spelling.
9.  Read the next page to see that the continuation is correct.
10. Go back to the first page and read silently from the bottom up to catch mistakes you might have overlooked.
11. Proofread at different levels. For example, read the headings and subheadings only, followed by the headers and footers only, followed by tables only, to check for correctness and consistency. Use the Proofreading Checklist to determine the levels you want to differentiate.
12. Proofread in spurts. Remember that your concentration level is likely to wane after 15 to 30 minutes.

## AFTER YOU PROOFREAD

13. Add to the Proofreading Checklist any new error types you have discovered. Say that subject-verb agreement is a common problem for you (e.g., writing "Bob or Tina do" instead of "Bob or Tina does"). Add this mistake to the list and start the discipline of looking out for the problem.
14. Correct the copy and save the file.
15. Print a fresh copy and find someone else who has not seen the document and who has a keen eye for detail and the time to proofread the copy.
16. If your second proofreader finds errors, correct them, save the new file, and print two new hard copies.

17. Find another person with a keen eye for detail and the time, and give this third proofreader one of your copies.
18. Have the third proofreader read the document aloud as you follow along by reading the text. (It may make more sense for the proofreader to read the copy aloud because he or she is more likely to stumble when encountering a mistake that you and the second proofreader overlooked.)
19. If either of you finds errors, correct the copy and save the file.
20. Print a fresh copy and scan the copy yourself one more time for printing quirks, blemishes, and ink quality.

Try your eye at proofreading by working on the memo in Exercise 6-1 on page 214. Go on a search-and-destroy mission by clearing the document of as many mistakes as you can find, and practice with the Proofreading Checklist and Proofreading Symbols.

## Summary

Proofreading is the third and final phase of Quality Controlling, Step 3 of the PDQ writing process. After revising and editing, careful on-the-job writers print a hard copy of their documents and search for mistakes they might have overlooked. They should follow the comprehensive Positive Proofreading Procedure, refer to the Proofreading Checklist, and use proofreading symbols.

# EXERCISE 6-1
# PROOFREADING

*Using proofreading symbols, correct the proofreading errors in the memo below.*

## MEMORANDUM

To: All Stuff

From:    Rex Montana

Date:    April 5, 2005

Re:    The Annual Fun Run in Central Park

The Fun Ran Committee met on April 4, 2004 and decided to share information about our annual event scheduled for Sunday, April 10, in Central Park.

### 1.    Volunteers

The Volunteer Subcommittee members are seeking at least 15 more volunteers to help at the event. We'll need two types of volunteers; registration helpers and security officers. If you're interested, please speak to any of the Volunteer Subcommittee members: Matt Demattis, Susan Piscatelli, Kyle, Ward, or Kerry Simonetti.

### 2.    Donations

This year, Susan Piscateli, the Donations Comittee Chairperson, has set the Fun Run fundraising goal of $25,000. In keeping with Company tradition of rotating event beneficiaries, Susan announced that proceeds from the event will go to The People's House. Please
send donations (cash or check only to Susan in Suite 16. You will receive a receipts for cash donations. Donations by check should be made payable to "MTC Fun Run Committee.

### Location, Time, and Distance

This year the sight of the fun run will be the Park Drive North at 72nd Street. (The path beginning at the boathouse was unavailable this year since we shifted the event top Saturday.) Runners should register no later then 8:30 a.m. the starter's gun will begin the race at 9:15 a.m. sharp. If you are running with a partner or a group, please register together. All running paris and groups will receive identical numberswith letter suffixes. The distance remains 5 kilometers.

### 4.    Awards

All runners will receive personalized citations. If you want the Committee to The Committee is always looking for ways to host a fun-filed, memorable party. Please submit any neat ideas to Sharon.

### 6.    Performing Guest

This year's special performing guest will be the Do Nots. They will perform at the conclusion of the race, approximately 11:00 a.m.

Please call me (X 109) or e-mail me (Rex.Montana@mtc.org) if you any questions about this year's big, fun-filed event. See you at the Fun Run!

# Proofreading Exercise Solution

## EXERCISE 6-1: PROOFREADING

**MEMORANDUM** *(underline)* *(ww)* *(align)*

To: All ~~Stuff~~ Staff
From: Rex Montana
Date: April 5, 2005    ←
Re: The Annual Fun Run in Central Park    *date? 2004 or 2005?*

The Fun Ran Committee met on April 4, 2004 and decided to share information about our annual event scheduled for Sunday, April 10, in Central Park.

### 1. Volunteers

The Volunteer Subcommittee members are seeking at least 15 more volunteers to help at the event We'll need two types of volunteers registration helpers and security officers. If you're interested, please speak to any of the Volunteer Subcommittee members: Matt Demattis, Susan Piscatelli, Kyle Ward, or Kerry Simonetti.

### 2. Donations    *Piscatelli spelling?*

This year, Susan Piscateli the Donations Comittee Chairperson, has set the Fun Run fundraising goal of $25,000. In keeping with Company tradition of rotating event beneficiaries, Susan announced that proceeds from the event will go to The People's House. Please send donations (cash or check only to Susan in Suite 16. You will receive a receipts for cash donations. Donations by check should be made payable to "MTC Fun Run Committee."

### 3. Location, Time, and Distance    *align*

This year the *site* ~~sight~~ of the fun run will be the Park Drive North at 72nd Street. (The path beginning at the boathouse was unavailable this year since we shifted the event to Saturday.) Runners should register no later then 8:30 a.m. the starter's gun will begin the race at 9:15 a.m. sharp. If you are running with a partner or a group, please register together. All running pairs and groups will receive identical numbers with letter suffixes. The distance remains 5 kilometers.

### 4. Awards

All runners will receive personalized citations. If you want the Committee to The Committee is always looking for ways to host a fun-filed, memorable party Please submit any neat ideas to Sharon.    *?what party?*    *?who's Sharon?*

### 6. Performing Guest

This year's special performing guest will be the Do Nots. They will perform at the conclusion of the race, approximately 11:00 a.m.

Please call me (X 109) or e-mail me (Rex.Montana@mtc.org) if you any questions about this year's big, fun-filed event. See you at the Fun Run!

*Keep consistent the font type, style, and size of heading.*

215

# Staying an On-the-Job Writer

"True ease in writing comes from art, not chance,
As those move easiest who have learned to dance."

– Alexander Pope,
*An Essay on Criticism*

∽

"If you would not be forgotten,
As soon as you are dead and rotten,
Either write things worthy reading,
Or do things worth the writing."

– Benjamin Franklin,
*Epitaph on Himself*

This chapter describes what we've covered in *The Art of On-the-Job Writing* and what remains in your continued commitment to excellent on-the-job writing. It summarizes the key points of the writing process and writing product, and it suggests ways to keep developing your writing.

## What We've Covered

I ended the first chapter of this book by asking you to complete the On-the-Job Writing Process/Product Checklist. If you completed it, read this book, and tried some of the exercises, return to that checklist. Now answer the following questions:

1. Would you be able to define these five terms: *process, statement, support, structure,* and *style*?
2. Are all the statements in the "Quality" column clear to you?
3. Would you now rate yourself better in any of the qualities?
4. If you rate yourself better in some of the qualities, do you notice that the strength lies in a particular domain?

5. Have you made any progress toward achieving the writing goals you set for yourself?
6. Do you see any remaining weaknesses?
7. If you do, do you notice that the weakness lies in a particular domain?

Having read this book, you should consider now an ideal time to decide what's next for you as a business or technical writer. No doubt about it: Whether you're moving up the corporate ladder or growing your own business, you will have to write more as time goes on. Your writing will speak for you in your absence. It will tell your organization, manager, subordinates, clients, and vendors what you think and how you think. Therefore, you will want your writing to sound as professional as your speaking. This means being purposeful, complete, organized, clear, concise, courteous, consistent, and correct. Let's take a few moments to recall the twelve key ideas in this book.

## CHAPTER 1

1. *Writing is a process as well as a product.* Mastering the process will make your writing efficient; mastering the product will make your writing effective.

2. *The PDQ writing process comprises:*
    · *planning*, when we brainstorm and organize ideas focused on our purpose and audience
    · *drafting*, when we write a rough copy from beginning to end
    · *quality controlling*, when we protect our r-e-p by revising, editing, and proofreading
   We need to use the entire writing process for challenging documents.

3. *The 4S Plan writing product includes:*
    · the *statement*, or purpose and next steps of the document
    · the *support*, which addresses the reader's concerns related to the purpose
    · the *structure*, or organization and format, of the statement and support
    · the style, another word for the balancing of *content* and *context* language in the document

All four elements work harmoniously to guide your readers in capturing your ideas as you intend.

## CHAPTER 2

4. *We plan our documents before drafting to generate ideas and to overcome writing process problems. Those problems include:*
   - writer's block
   - procrastination
   - stress
   - poor time management
   - insecurity

5. *We plan by establishing the 3 A's of the document:*
   - the *aim,* or purpose of the document
   - the *audience,* or primary and secondary readers of the document
   - the *area,* or scope of the document

6. *Among the techniques available for planning the document are these six:*
   - *boilerplate,* appropriate text from previous documents to be used for jumpstarting the writing process
   - *planning template,* a customized outlining tool centered around the 3 A's
   - *audience surveys,* a self-generated questionnaire containing issues your readers are likely to want addressed about your topic
   - *idea lists,* a structured brainstorming and organizing technique used on a blank computer screen or sheet of paper
   - *idea tags,* a group of post-its or index cards each listing one idea specific to your topic
   - *idea maps,* a free-form illustrating technique to tap into your creativity as you reflect on your topic

## CHAPTER 3

7. *The goal of drafting is quantity, not quality.* To ensure our drafts are thorough, we should:
   - feel free to ramble

- let serendipity happen
- commit everything to paper and nothing to memory

8. *The four requirements for drafting are:*
   - finding a comfortable place
   - choosing a protected time
   - using a preferred writing tool
   - writing without pause

## CHAPTER 4

9. *We revise mindful at all times of our purpose and audience.* They are the keys to quality controlling on-the-job documents.

10. *When revising, we CARE*: change, add, reorganize/reformat, and eliminate ideas.

## CHAPTER 5

11. *When editing, we check the expression of language.* This includes:
    - sentence structure, conciseness, voice, and tone
    - grammar and word usage
    - punctuation and mechanics

## CHAPTER 6

12. *When proofreading, we check a hard copy for overlooked mistakes* by using:
    - a proofreading checklist containing the most frequently overlooked errors
    - proofreading symbols, which are understood universally by experienced proofreaders
    - the positive proofreading procedure to ensure we miss nothing

So much goes into the preparation, development, and improvement of on-the-job documents. This book encapsulates much of that work. It is the result of reviewing, assessing, writing, or editing thousands of business and technical e-mails, memos, letters, reports, proposals, procedures, policies, and white papers for more than 25 years. Despite its usefulness as a reference source, however, this book cannot do the writing for you. Different writing situations demand different approaches: establishing different purposes, reaching different audiences, addressing different concerns, employing different organization techniques, choosing different styles. A lot of thinking goes into excellent writing.

## What Remains

Now that you have invested so much of your valuable time into writing improvement, you will want to continue in the right direction. So here are 12 points to bear in mind as you move on toward writing mastery.

1. *Be confident.* In the words of filmmaker and comedian Woody Allen, "eighty percent of success is showing up." If you're still holding on to your job or business, or if you have solid prospects for a new venture, you must be doing some things right. Know what those things are and build on them. Then use them when you approach your writing tasks.

2. *Practice.* Mastering the techniques in this book requires repeated application. Think of your on-the-job writing as a *practice*, in the way physicians and lawyers consider their work a practice. Seek writing opportunities at work whenever you can—even those that seem exceedingly difficult. This spirit of diligence will take you far toward winning those writing assignments your managers or clients need accomplished. The German philosopher Friedrich Nietzsche once said, "It takes less time to learn how to write nobly than how to write lightly and straightforwardly." The play that takes you two hours to see takes the actors hundreds of hours to rehearse. Similarly, what takes your reader moments to read should take you far more time to produce.

3. *Keep a notebook.* Take a notebook with you wherever you go: the train, doctor's waiting room, supermarket, bank, post office, restaurant—especially those places where you have to wait in line. Use that dead time to take notes. You'll never know when a creative idea will surface, but with your notebook around you'll have a better chance of retaining it. Your notebook can be of the electronic or paper sort—whichever is more convenient and conducive to writing. You may use it as a life diary, a record of business events, an inventory of your creative ideas,

whatever. The important thing is not *what* you write so much as *that* you write. Free writing keeps the brain and fingers freshly connected in this mental and physical activity. Do it for the same reason that you would work out at the gym: to stay in shape.

4. *Collect samples.* Collect good writing samples. If you read some document on the job that strikes you as a model of good writing, keep a copy of it. Study what makes it so effective. For sure, it would have something to do with the statement, support, structure, and style. Make a folder of all the excellent models you have collected. Categorize them by type: requests, responses, reports, proposals, meeting minutes, root-cause analyses, policies, procedures, and so on. Since the company owns these models, you should feel free to copy ideas from them when they are relevant to your document. Copying models of excellence is the way we all learned to talk and write. After you've borrowed an idea here and there from this or that document, you'll be on your way to emulating those ideas in your own documents.

5. *Read.* Good writers read a lot; in fact, reading material is the writer's food. While not all good readers are good writers, all good writers are good readers. They know what good writers do to clarify meaning for their readers and to inspire them to action. Always have two books and two magazines in your current reading: one in your field, and one outside your field. The one in your field will keep you abreast of the technical aspects related to your profession; the one outside your field will expand your viewpoint and build your vocabulary. As for what to read outside your field, it doesn't matter—so long as the writing is of a high caliber. Choose topics of interest to you: history, fashion, economics, biology, religion, astronomy, military, agriculture, music, art, theater, home repair, automobiles. This is a fun way to broaden your knowledge base, learn new words, and bring fresh viewpoints into the problems you deal with at work.

6. *Learn.* Realizing that you write as you speak, start owning the new words you read by writing them down on post-its or index

cards, keeping them as bookmarks so they'll be nearby, and using them in your daily conversations. Begin adding these words to your writing vocabulary. (Caution: Do not commit the tone problem of ostentation by writing *insipid* when *dull* would do. As the French philosopher Jean De La Bruyère said, "the noblest deeds are well enough set forth in simple language.") Write those words in your drafts if they fit the message. Who knows? Maybe you'll coin a new term for your department or field. While you're at it, keep handy a few good unabridged and current reference books: a dictionary, thesaurus, and grammar and stylebook, all recently published. Many options are available at your local bookstore or online.

7. *Talk writing.* Make writing a topic of your workplace conversation. This does not mean just *talk* and not *write*. After all, Nietzsche also said, "The author must keep his mouth shut when his work starts to speak." However, engineers talk about engineering problems, auditors about auditing problems, and nurses about nursing problems. If writing is an important part of your job, then talk with your teammates about writing problems. You may learn that they face the same problem or, better yet, that they have learned to overcome the problem or to compensate for it. Meanwhile, you are teaching as much as you are learning by raising communication issues of common concern that affect the business.

8. *Read writers.* Read what experts have to say about the writing process. Articles, books, and websites abound on the subject. Learn what professionals do to stay creative, meet deadlines, and enjoy what they do.

9. *Set goals.* Write down specific deadlines for completing those reports, proposals, and company newsletter articles you've committed to. Also set standards that you want to reach, say, four new ideas per year all presented in proposal form, or one new marketing slide presentation per quarter, or ten e-mail responses per day. But be realistic. Do not set unreachable goals. Track your record at meeting those deadlines and reward yourself when you do. When you don't, figure out why and don't give up. Simply adjust the standard and reset the goal—then go for it.

10. *Expect mistakes.* Know that errors are a part of the writing business. As long as you haven't yet sent out the document, you can still work toward perfecting it.

11. *Seek feedback.* Make pacts with teammates stating that you will edit or proofread each other's documents. Being thin-skinned will do you no good. Accept editorial advice from your manager—and even subordinates—as commentary not intended to demoralize you but to improve your communication.

12. *Remember the purpose-audience connection.* You need to know your readers as well as your subject matter; therefore, *context* matters as much as *content*. Write to your readers the way you would speak to them when you are at your professional best.

There you have it: the art of on-the job writing, a means by which you use the writing process to improve the writing product, in which you integrate purpose and audience, balance content and context, and realize the continuum of self-improvement through powerful use of language. Excellent writing comes from hard work, so get started.

# ABOUT THE AUTHOR

Philip Vassallo has taught college-level writing for over 25 years, evaluated the writing of thousands of professionals across the entire spectrum of the corporate hierarchy, and developed and delivered writing training programs for a wide range of administrative, technical, and managerial professionals in corporate and government environments throughout the United States. He has also provided individualized writing coaching and assessment services for numerous corporate employees. Phil writes *Words on the Line*, a column on effective writing for *ETC: A Review of General Semantics*, the journal of the Institute of General Semantics, of which he has been a member since 1990. As an essayist and poet, he has contributed to numerous print and electronic publications throughout the world, and as a playwright, he has seen ten of his plays produced. He holds a bachelor's degree in English from Baruch College, a master's in education from Lehman College, and a doctorate in educational theory from Rutgers University.

# Do your employees need a writing workshop? They do!

More than ever, employees face the challenging task of writing on demand in dynamic work situations. In a service economy, global environment, and information age, ideas lead to results. Driven by this powerful reality, businesses must communicate purposefully, consultatively, and ethically to fulfill their clients' needs and to guide their operations.

For many years, Philip Vassallo has designed, led, and supervised writing courses to support administrative, technical, and sales professionals from numerous Fortune 500 companies, government agencies, and nonprofit organizations. Dr. Vassallo offers classroom-style, computer-lab, and online versions of his unique writing program, providing personalized feedback and engendering learning experiences that are enjoyable, interactive, collaborative, challenging, and relevant.

Courses include:

**General Writing Courses**
Business Writing for Results
Write to the Point
Writing Effective E-mail
Persuasive Writing
Customer Service Writing

**Technical Writing Courses**
Effective Technical Writing
Standard Operating Procedures
Technical Proposals
Technical Reports
Technical Research Articles

**Editing Courses**
English for Nonnative Employees
Revising, Editing, and Proofreading
Business Grammar

**Specialized Documents Courses**
Writing Winning Proposals
Writing Executive Summaries
Writing for Financial Professionals
Writing for Auditors
Writing Evaluation Reports
Writing Meeting Minutes

To take the first step toward developing your employees' writing skills, contact Dr. Vassallo today at 503-968-6777 or vassallo@firstbooks.com.

# First Books®
# Order Form

**FIRST BOOKS®** RELOCATION AND BUSINESS RESOURCES

| NEWCOMER'S HANDBOOKS | # COPIES | TOTAL |
|---|---|---|
| Newcomer's Handbook® for Atlanta | _____ x $24.95 | $_____ |
| Newcomer's Handbook® for Boston | _____ x $23.95 | $_____ |
| Newcomer's Handbook® for Chicago | _____ x $21.95 | $_____ |
| Newcomer's Handbook® for London | _____ x $20.95 | $_____ |
| Newcomer's Handbook® for Los Angeles | _____ x $23.95 | $_____ |
| Newcomer's Handbook® for Minneapolis-St. Paul | _____ x $20.95 | $_____ |
| Newcomer's Handbook® for New York City | _____ x $22.95 | $_____ |
| Newcomer's Handbook® for San Francisco | _____ x $20.95 | $_____ |
| Newcomer's Handbook® for Seattle | _____ x $21.95 | $_____ |
| Newcomer's Handbook® for Washington D.C. | _____ x $21.95 | $_____ |
| Newcomer's Handbook® for the USA | _____ x $23.95 | $_____ |
| The Moving Book: A Kids' Survival Guide | _____ x $20.95 | $_____ |
| The Pet-Moving Handbook | _____ x $ 9.95 | $_____ |

| FIRST BOOKS TRAINING LIBRARY | | |
|---|---|---|
| The Art of On-the-Job Writing | _____ x $21.95 | $_____ |
| Pass the 6 | _____ x $49.95 | $_____ |
| Pass the 63 | _____ x $35.95 | $_____ |
| | **SUBTOTAL** | $_____ |
| **US POSTAGE AND HANDLING** (*$7.00 first book, $1.50 each add'l.*) | | $_____ |
| | **TOTAL** | $_____ |

SHIP TO:

Name _____

Title _____

Company _____

Address _____

City _____ State _____ Zip/Postal Code _____

Country _____

Phone _____

*Allow 1-2 weeks for delivery*

Order on our website (www.firstbooks.com), or send this order form and a check or money order payable to:
First Books
6750 SW Franklin St., Suite A
Portland, OR 97223-2542
USA